A Guiding Light:
Poems and Reflections

A work of the Holy Spirit speaking words of
comfort, encouragement, and instruction

Corliss Udoema

Author	Corliss Udoema, Haymarket, VA
Publisher	**MMGI** B O O K S
ISBN	ISBN-13: 978-1939774293 ISBN-10: 1939774292
Cover Art	2016©; Photo Credit Title Page: Corliss Udoema Public Domain Image / Cover: FreeImages.com/AndrewKlaus

Author:	You may contact the author with questions or comments at: aguidinglight2u@gmail.com or www.corlissudoema.com

Table of Contents

To Readers

As God has led me in writing each poem, may the words be a light and an inspiration to you. May you also be blessed to receive a special word from God.

The Lord has blessed me with a great and wonderful life. As I continue this journey, I desire to let my light so shine before men that they may see my good works and glorify my Father which is in heaven. I pray continuously to always be a blessing to others as I share the love of God. May my life and my poems be a living testimony of God's grace and mercy. May we remember our faith in He who set the captives free, and know that because of the love that Jesus has for us, all things are possible. As a minister of God's word, I pray continually without ceasing for you.

God bless you for choosing to read, *A Guiding Light: Poems and Reflections.* In the name of Jesus, my prayer is you will be blessed and inspired.

God has given me a message of hope, encouragement, and salvation through poetic praise. He has lovingly spoken to my heart, and I bless His Holy name. Thank you, God, for sending your son, Jesus, so there is a message to tell, and a hallelujah thank you for the Holy Spirit that teaches me and brings all things that you have spoken to my remembrance. I give honor and praise to my Lord and Savior, Jesus Christ, who is the head of my life and the author and finisher of my faith. Thank you, Lord, I am delivered, set apart, and blessed to run the race. You have given me a measure of faith and promised a reward if I faint not. Lord, I thank you for giving me a word to speak – in and out of season. Now beloved, take a moment, and read what God has spoken to me. From my heart to yours, I hope that you will be blessed. For each of the poems, I have included scriptures that inspired my writings, as well as my personal reflections.

May the Lord engulf you in His love and reveal His message in each of the poems. I pray you will remember and reflect on your

own starting point in this wonderful walk of salvation. May the Holy Spirit minister to you if you uncover hurtful things in your past that have not healed. I decree and declare in the mighty, majestic, and holy name of Jesus that you are set free, delivered and healed. If you are reading this book and do not know the Lord Jesus as your personal savior, the Lord
is calling you to repent. Romans 10:9-10 says 'If thou shall confess with thy mouth the Lord Jesus, and shall believe in thine heart that God hath raised him from the dead thou shalt be saved. For with the heart man believeth unto righteousness; and with the mouth confession is made unto salvation. Tell the Lord that you are a sinner and desire a place with Him in paradise. You can be a new creature in Christ, no longer bound in sin.'
Repeat the words of the sinner's prayer with your heart:

"Lord, I am a sinner. I confess with my mouth that I am a sinner and repent of my sins. I believe that Jesus died for me and that on the third day He rose with all power in His hands I believe that by the blood of Jesus my sins are forgiven.

Lord, I give my life to you. From this day forward, my life belongs to you and I am no longer a sinner but saved by grace. I pray this prayer in Jesus' name. Amen."

If you have prayed this prayer, let me welcome you to the family of our Lord and Savior Jesus Christ. Let the words herein be a pathway to higher peace, joy and understanding.

Beloved in the Lord, may you be led deeper and deeper into His peace, His love, His grace and, His mercy.

I love you all in the name of Jesus.

With Love,

Corliss Udoema

Dedication & Acknowledgements

This book is dedicated to memory of my late father, James 'Pediac' Pearson, and mother, Dorothy Bell (Dot) Pearson. Thank you for choosing me at the age of six months to be your child. You had all the choices in the world, but you chose me! Thank you. I shall always remember you!

All my love and appreciation to family and friends that enriched my life. To my children, grandchildren, and great grandchildren by birth and by love you make my heart smile! Andrea, Andrew, Bianca, Danielle, Donna, Robyn, Angela, Tony, Armand, Dave, Darryl, Wayne, Tracy, Verna, Jan, Regina, Bill (B3), James, Randall, William, Vaughn, Kip, Sascha, Pat, Terronda, Chris, Diane and Scott. To my great granddaughter, Annelise, you are Gigi's 'baby, baby, baby, my beautiful baby!' Victoria

Grace, my second granddaughter, you came reminding all of us of that His victory and His grace are all that we need.

To the late, Daniel Akan Udoema … you taught me your Yoruba culture, shared your love, and ultimately your name … 'Udo-ema' the one who is loved.

I offer my loving gratitude to Bishop Jesse L. Williams. Your anointing is awesome Bishop. Continue to press on for the prize. I will always love you and never forget you.

Peace and blessings to my pastor, Dr. Eugene Johnson, fellow ministers in the gospel at Mt. Olive Baptist Church and my church family at Mt. Olive Baptist Church, Centerville, Virginia.

A warm remembrance of my Tres Dias family, Decolores in Japan, and around the world. Lord, keep Your hand on my home church, Mt. Calvary Missionary Baptist Church in New Bern, North Carolina.

To my sisters whom God has healed and delivered from breast cancer, I love you. Reverend Rose McElrath-Slade, you are indeed an awesome warrior for the Lord. Your testimony is inspiring and encouraging. You will always be my sister in love.

To my sisters healed on the other side of Jordan, we miss you and shall forever cherish your memory. See you around the throne on that day we shall all be changed. Sister Churchill, you were a rock! Nancy Speed, your legacy of love continues to shine in our hearts and in our lives.

My Inspiration for: A Man

He is the kind of man you will find praying and studying the word of God. You know him as a man whose steps are ordered by God. His family respects him for being a Godly man. He takes on the nature of Nehemiah as the leader of his family. He shows leadership in his church and in his community. He has the faith of Abraham, believing that what God says, 'He is able to perform it.' He takes on the courage of David, because he knows it is not what is in his hands that gives him the victory, but whose hands he is in. He has the determination of Jacob, saying, "God I won't let go until you bless me." He has the 'waiting' power of Moses, knowing 40 years is not too long to wait to do the work God has called him to do! Mighty men of God, holdfast to your faith and be blessed as you read *A Man*.

This poem is dedicated to Bishop Jessie Williams, Pastor, and teacher … in the 'church without walls', and my granddaddy, the late Deacon Ossie Andrews.

A Man

A man of honor
And a man of goodness I long to be
When I look in the mirror
A man of truth and justice I pray to see

A man who builds bridges of understanding
And seeks to make peace in every way
A man who in love serves as head of his
household
Each and every day

A man who loves God
With his soul, heart and mind
A man who for God's sake
Is gentle, meek and kind

A man who knows that all he is
And ever hopes to be
Is what God whispers in his ear
As he bows down on bended knee

A man who presses for the prize
And never gives up the fight
A man whose steps are ordered by God
Determined to do what is right

A man who fasts and prays
Because this is God's command
A man who leans not to his own ways
Because he knows it is on God's promises
That he must stand

A man who God has given authority
Over the air, sea and land
A man who is not afraid
To humble himself before God's almighty
hand

A man who never ceases to praise God
And bless His Holy Name
A man that openly cries out to his father
Tears flow yet he has no shame

A man who knows that what he sows
He shall also reap
A man that knows it is not his plan
But the masters that he must keep

A man who is found faithful
At the beginning and ending of each day
A man who never forgets to thank God
For just one more chance to pray.

*Corinthians 15:58 (King James Version)
Therefore, my beloved brethren, be ye
stedfast, unmoveable, always abounding in
the work of the Lord, forasmuch as ye know
that your labour is not in vain in the Lord.*

My Inspiration for: A Woman

The woman is a neighbor that always opens her heart and doors to the needy. You can easily recognize her as the woman who always freely gives to others. She is the faithful woman of God who is always there with a heart full of love and compassion for others.

Who is this remarkable woman of God?

I am sure you know her. Maybe you call her Mom, mother, mama, or mommy. Perhaps her name is grandma, granny, gammy, mama, big mama, or Nona. She could be called wife, sis, auntie, or cousin.

The woman could be called Anna. She is the mighty woman of prayer that never tired of being in His presence. The woman that sat outside the gates, but who knew her place was wherever Jesus was.

The woman could be called Esther. She

was a woman who was determined to seek audience with the King. A woman of courage and direction who went covered with prayer and fasting and stated, "if I perish, I perish, I am going to see the king."

The woman could be called Ruth. A woman of loyalty and faithfulness whose alliance and allegiance was not based on situations or circumstances. She was a woman who tirelessly gleaned in the hot sun to bring food for her family. She was the woman who lovingly stood by her mother-in-law despite Naomi's situation.

The woman may be nameless like the woman from Samaria, or the Shulamite woman, the woman with the issue of blood, or the widow woman.

The woman may be Doris, Mary, Mary Ann, Mary Lou, Betty, Betty Lou, Mildred, Niyi, Miriam, Michellina, Nevada, Marilyn, Augustine, Arletta, Lolita, Loretta, Sheryl, Robyn, Vercella, Vicky, Lori, Sherry, Shirley, Diane, Shelia, Charlene, Barbara, Lydia, Sharon, Claudine, Annette, Dawn, Yvonne, Simone, Vilma, Teresa, Terry, Leticia, Helen, Tiffany, Carmen, Tammy, Estelle, Janet, Seretha, Drusilla, Lois, Dorothy, Essie Lee,

Vanessa, Alice, Vivian, Andrea, Lula, Donna, Mollie, June, Emogene, Carolyn, Marie, Tanya, Martha, Linda, Willette, Mervene, Shaila, Shanna, Sarah, Denise, Angela, Mabel, Lurlie, Danielle, Jeannette, Ileana, Wynester, Kim, Pam, Debbie, Rose, Yasko, Abe, Modupe, Femi, Joan, Joanne, Cynthia, Sandra, Bianca, Danielle, Joyce, Susan, Rebbeca, Marlo, Regina, Claudia, Elsa, Carolina, Elizabeth, Tina, Fern, Jackie, Ann, Claudette, Bobbie, Dorice, Zhihony, Ernise, Patti, Patricia, Polly, Novella, Fay, or the woman may be YOU! Be blessed as you read *A Woman*.

    This poem is dedicated to Brenda Carradine, Co-Pastor of International Harvest Christian Fellowship Church and author of 'Lady Preacher.' Brenda Carradine is a mighty woman of God who is tireless in her efforts to preach the word of God.

A Woman

A woman of honor
And a woman of grace I long to be
When I look in the mirror
A woman of love and kindness I pray to see

A woman who shares with others
And has an encouraging word to say
A woman who will work
While it is still day

A woman who fears God
And always seeks His favor
A woman that never tires
Of doing God's labor

A woman who goes to the well
In the heat of the day
A woman who clings to Jesus
And remembers to watch as well as pray

A woman who joyfully shares
What salvation is all about
A woman that touches the heart of many
And trusts God without doubt

A woman who stretches out
Her hands to those in need
A woman who will always reap
Because she knows the value of one seed!

Proverbs 31:20 (King James Version)
She stretcheth out her hand to the poor; yea,
she reacheth forth her hands to the needy.

My Inspiration for: Crossroads

Many times, in life, you reach a crossroad … a decision on what direction you will take. Sometimes it can be a simple matter of deciding where you will go for dinner or what outfit you will wear. However, it could be a life changing decision of choosing to accept the Lord. God has given us all free will.

We can choose to serve Him and walk in the light or we can choose to live in a life of eternal darkness. When we make Jesus our choice, we choose to live a life that shows the world we are a child of the Most-High King.

Crossroads is a poem inspired by one woman's struggle to overcome an alcohol addiction. Once this woman walked in the spirit of Philippians 4:13, and said, "I can do all things through Christ who strengthens me," her addiction was conquered – in the name of Jesus.

Whatever the addiction, God has sent His son to rescue us and set us free. Be blessed as you read *Crossroads*.

This poem is dedicated to all those that have suffered, battled and conquered addictions. Through our Lord and Savior Jesus Christ, they found they were more than conquerors.

Crossroads

One foot out
And, one foot in
Hiding in the shadows
 Living in sin

Day-to-day struggle
To keep it all together
No umbrella in sight
For all this stormy weather

I know about the one
Who died for you and me
But my addiction is so strong
It can't be broken you see

I know the right way to go
And the right thing to do
I know I need to let go
And say God, I'm depending on You

Don't look at me like that
If I take a little drink every now and then
Just show me in the Bible
Where I'm committing a sin

A witness for Him
In all that I do and say
Be clean, fast
And go down on my knees to pray

Lord look down
On a tormented soul like me
Purge me with hyssop, wash me
Make me who You want me to be

Strengthen my weak spirit
So, I will stop hiding my light under the bed
Set my feet on a righteous path
I have not forgotten that on Calvary You bled

You didn't die on the cross for me to sit down
And waste my life away
You did it so that I would have the power
To overcome satan, each and every day

Stand up, shake it off
start living for the Holy One
Stand up, shake it off
My new life has begun!

Romans 8:37 (King James Version)
Nay, in all these things we are more than
conquerors through him that loved us.

My Inspiration for: Fight for Your Destiny

The inspiration for this poem came from a sermon preached by Dr. Alice Hooker, Pastor of Works for Christ Christian Center, Sanford, North Carolina. Dr. Hooker preached about the eagle and the crow. Dr. Hooker spoke of these two birds relative to reaching our destiny.

She explained, "As born again believers, we are the eagles. The crow is the enemy that likes to frustrate our purpose and our destiny. As we move toward our destiny the crow pursues and attempts to overtake us."

"As eagles," Dr. Hooker said, "we should continue to fly higher and higher in the Lord; the crow will soon reach a level where he will no longer be able to breathe, and therefore cannot continue to fly higher."

I have a visual of that old crow running out of breath and coughing; trying to pursue

us. On the other hand, we – like the eagle –
can soar to great heights. Dr. Hooker said
whenever we are going to a higher level in the
Lord, the crow will always try to follow and
distract us, but we must continue to soar
higher and higher in the Lord. Praise God
from whom all blessings flow!

As you begin or continue your walk with
the Lord, it is so wonderful 'to know that we
know that we know'; we can soar like an
eagle. Soar and be blessed as you read *Fight
for Your Destiny*.

This poem is dedicated to Dr. Alice
Hooker, a woman who has taken on the
nature of the eagle and continues to soar
higher and higher in the Lord.

Fight for Your Destiny

Fighting the good fight of faith
Is impossible for you to do
If you leave all your faith
And power on the church pew

Don't let your spiritual armor
Sit around and collect dust
Don't hold on to your problems
Just pray God … it is You that I trust

Preacher already told you
That old crow can't bring you down
So why is your head hanging low
And on your face I see a big frown

You are the eagle
So just spread your wings and go higher
That old crow can't follow you
He's out of breath and you know the devil is a
liar

It's time to walk in power
And fight for your destiny
The victory is won
Every time you go down on your knee

It's time to walk in power
And fight for your destiny
The battle is the Lord's
It is He that has set you free

It's time to walk in power
And fight for your destiny
Don't wait for the battle to be over
Shout hallelujah now and claim the victory!

Isaiah 40:31 (King James Version)
But they that wait upon the Lord shall renew
their strength; they shall mount up with wings
as eagles; they shall run, and not be weary;
and they shall walk, and not faint.

My Inspiration for: From Me to You

How many times has someone done something for you and you thought to yourself 'that was truly special?' The beauty of love and friendship compels us to think of ways to express how much we care. However, in our fast-paced world, we often rush from one place to another trying to accomplish so many things during our waking hours that many times we don't take time to say thank you.

One day I took the time to select a 'Thank You' card because it occurred to me that I too had not taken *time* to say thank you. As I began reading the cards, it crossed my mind how many languages I could say thank you.

English of course, Italian, Spanish, German, Swahili, Polish, Japanese, Korean, Yoruba, and Tagalog. However, if it were possible to say thank you in all the languages of the world, it would not be enough to express the love and thanksgiving for special people like you...my family and my friends. May the Lord bless you as you read From Me to You.

This poem is dedicated to those who are a blessing in my life. Maybe you prayed for me, maybe you called, maybe you sent an email or a text, maybe you visited me, maybe you brought me a meal, maybe you did a home repair, maybe you gave me a smile, maybe you gave me an encouraging word, maybe you wiped my tears, maybe you held my hand or maybe you gave me a much-needed hug. Whatever you did, this is for you; thank you and God bless you!

From Me to You

A moment my friend to share
Some words straight from my heart
Thank you for your thoughtfulness
But this is only a start

You always make me feel special
In even the little things that you do
Acts of kindness and love
That could only come from you

Words to describe how you've blessed me
I cannot even find
So, I'll just close my note and say
Thank you for being a special friend of mine!

John 13:34 (King James Version)
A new commandment I give unto you; That ye love one another; as I have loved you, that ye also love one another.

My Inspiration for: I Am

I was witnessing to a friend about riding through the storms of life. It is easier to tell someone to ride it out than to do it yourself.

You know, by faith, God is able to do it. Yet, sometimes you do not have the faith to convince yourself that God WILL do it. When you hear the wind, and see its fury, it is hard to stand in the eye of the storm. You say the words, "I have a God that can, and will, deliver me"; yet your faith is running low and you are struggling with doubt.

As I was sharing words to encourage my friend, God spoke into my spirit, and said tell him to put on his garment of praise. I then remembered a sermon by my pastor, Dr. Eugene Johnson, Mt. Olive Baptist Church in Centerville, Virginia. Pastor Johnson told us a secret ... what to do when we are in the midst of a storm.

He told us to get a piece of paper and write down ALL of the challenges we felt were too many to count, ALL of the mountains we felt were too high to climb, ALL of the valleys we felt were too deep to cross, ALL of the disappointments we felt were too great to endure, ALL of the hurts we felt were too hard to bear and ALL of the weights we felt were too heavy to carry.

Next go to our favorite room and put on our favorite praise song. Take the piece of paper that lists ALL of the challenges, all of the mountains, all of the valleys, all of the disappointments, all of the hurts and all of the weights and throw it on the floor and praise our way through it as you we dance like David danced before the Lord. Pastor Johnson, thank you … now the secret is out!

Yes, Lord, regardless of what is going on in my life, when I praise You, I know that you are a very present help in the time of trouble. When I am weak then I am strong. When I am broken and hurting, I know You are close because You draw nigh to those of a broken heart and a contrite spirit. In Your word you comfort me and let me know You inhabit the praise of your people. Be blessed as you read *I Am*.

This poem is dedicated to those standing in a storm. I am praying you have put on your garment of praise and you ARE praising your way through the storm!

I Am

I am standing on the rock of salvation
I am riding through my storm
I am destined and determined to make it
The enemy can do me no harm

I am claiming victory in Jesus
I am taking possession of the land
I am fixed and planted where He wants me
God's purpose is clear to understand

I am putting on my garment of praise
I am thanking Him with all my heart
I am walking in blessed assurance
I am vowing to do my part!

Psalm 91:2 (King James Version)
I will say of the LORD, He is my refuge and
my fortress: my God; in him will I trust.

My Inspiration for: I Am Persuaded

Every time I think about the song *Standing on the Promises*, I think about Doris Richardson Felder, my friend, my godmother, and a mighty woman of God. Doris loves to sing 'standing on the promises of Christ my savior'; and she lives what she sings. Through trials and tribulations, Doris will smile even if she must smile though tears and say, "I am standing on the promises."

Doris is a woman who raised two sons, five granddaughters and two adopted daughters. Doris is indeed a special woman. Whenever there is a need in the community, you can be assured Doris will be one of the first to respond. A caring and compassionate woman of God, Doris is a blessing in the lives of all who know her. She can be found standing on the promises, because for her it is not just a song, but a way of life.

I believe to stand on the promises of God, you must trust God and to trust God you must know God. I love the most famous rhetorical question in the Bible … is there anything too hard for God? Of course, we all know the answer is no. There is nothing too hard for God. God said He would not have His word return void, that what He sent it to do, that it will accomplish. Be blessed as you stand on the promises of God and read *I Am Persuaded*.

This poem is dedicated to Doris Richardson Felder and the beautiful people of Rocky Run community in New Bern, North Carolina, who long ago decided to stand on the promises of God.

I Am Persuaded

I am persuaded
That God will do
Exactly what He said
He would do

I am persuaded that all power
Is in His hands
That God sent His son
In the flesh, just like mans

I am persuaded in the ninth hour
When He gave up the ghost
That He gave His life
Leaving no room for satan to boast

The prophecy said
That no bones would be broken
And it was fulfilled
Just as God had spoken

The longer I live
And the more I grow in grace
I realize how much
I long to see Jesus face to face

In a building not made by hands
One day we'll rest
And the work we've done
Will be put in the fire to test

I am persuaded
That we should live a life that is holy
Remembering always
To approach the throne of grace boldly

I am persuaded neither life nor death
Will separate me from the love of God
I am persuaded
That over the enemy I have the power to trod

I am persuaded
That what God promised He is able to do
Oh, what precious promises
For me and for you

It is on God's promises
That I do stand
Because you see
I am persuaded that yes God can!

Romans 4:20-21 (King James Version)
He staggered not at the promise of God
through unbelief; but was strong in faith,
giving glory to God; And being fully persuaded
that, what he had promised, he was able also
to perform.

My Inspiration for: I See a Rainbow

No matter how old I am, I will never stop being excited when I see a rainbow. Over the years, I have pulled off the highway, gotten out of my car and jumped with joy when I have seen a rainbow. Sometimes I will just stand and look at the rainbow or at other times I will try to hold on to the memory by taking a picture. We transition from the beauty of the rainbow to the turn of events that challenged me to remember the rainbow. My situation came about suddenly and without warning.

After 30 years of working for the federal government and always receiving my paycheck on time, something unthinkable happened! I received a paycheck for a two-week period; however, the amount did not even cover two hours of my salary! Over the next several weeks, my paycheck was continually several thousand dollars short. Let me say, the human side of me surfaced, and I was not happy.

I found myself like the Israelites, grumbling and complaining about all the things going wrong in my life. Failure to get a full pay check was only one of them. After several weeks (which seemed like months to me), I left my office one evening particularly disturbed about all the things going wrong in my life. To make matters worse, it seemed there was no sense of urgency on anyone's part to resolve my problems.

On my way home, I decided to stop by the grocery store to pick up a few essential items which consisted of comfort food – ice cream. I waited impatiently in line while the cashier rang up and packed my items. I found myself thinking … how long is this going to take? My ice cream will melt before the cashier can place my items in the bag!

In the middle of my 'pity party,' God spoke into my spirit and said, 'you are truly blessed. In fact, even though you have not been paid a full salary for several weeks, you have money to meet your needs and your wants. You have food. You are living rent free in a beautiful condo on the beach. You have been given a car to drive and you don't even have to pay for the gas. In fact, Corliss, you are so blessed right now, you should bless someone else!'

No one puts us where we belong quicker than the Holy Spirit. As I said a silent prayer, asking God to forgive me, my watering eyes focused on an elderly man standing behind me. I turned around and started helping him unload his cart. Looking at the number of items in his cart, he appeared to be shopping for the month. As I helped him, I felt such shame for my complaints. After his items were unloaded, I quietly stood to the side and waited until the cashier gave him the total due

... $93.27. As I heard the amount, I stepped forward and paid with my credit card. The gentleman didn't speak English, but it was clear he was very confused, because he kept trying to pay the cashier. The cashier continued to speak to him in Spanish and pointed in my direction. He looked at me with a confused look on his face as if he was thinking, 'why would a stranger pay for my groceries?' The confused look then gave way to a big smile. I shall never forget the look of appreciation on the old man's face nor the appreciation I felt to God for speaking such a blessing into my spirit.

The next morning on my way to work, I was on top of the world, believing God at His word, knowing that all things work together for good to those that love the Lord and who are 'the called' according to His purpose. As I was nearing my office, suddenly I saw the most beautiful rainbow in my life! I pulled over to the side of the road and began to praise God for His promises. As tears washed my face, I began to say … "I see a rainbow way up in the sky above, God is remembering His promises and I am remembering His love!"

This poem is dedicated to the beautiful people of Puerto Rico. Your love of God, and the warm and loving ways you reach out to others is a blessing.

I See a Rainbow

I see a rainbow
way up the in the sky above
I know God is remembering His promise
and I am remembering His love

As I travel life's rugged roads
I see many things not right
Yet I know that joy comes in the morning
and that I must fight the good fight

God speaks to my heart
peace be still
I cling to His words
so that I can do His perfect will

The precious promises
of God always abide
And under the shadow of His wings
we do hide

All of the trouble
all of the strife
I have a promise
that God is in charge of my life

So, no matter how dark
the clouds seem to be
I know that my heavenly Father
is lovingly watching over me

I see a rainbow
way up in the sky above
God is remembering His promise
and I am remembering His love.

Genesis 9:13-15 (King James Version)
I do set my bow in the cloud, and it shall be for a
token of a covenant between me and the earth.
14 And it shall come to pass, when I bring a cloud
over the earth, that the bow shall be seen in the
cloud: 15 And I will remember my covenant,
which is between me and you and every living
creature of all flesh; and the waters shall no more
become a flood to destroy all flesh.

My Inspiration for: I Thought I Knew

We have heard many variations of these words. If you knew what I know, you wouldn't do that. If I knew then what I know now, I would do things differently. Some say hindsight is 20/20 because we can look back and see what we could not see when we were in the past. If we could see where we were going before we got there, maybe we wouldn't go.

Bishop Wilfret Johnson, Oakville Missionary Baptist Church, Belle Chasse, Louisiana, preached a profound sermon about *Upstream Downstream*. It was the story of how folks in a small town had gotten together and were complaining about how much money was being wasted to pay a man that worked on the top of the hill. It seemed the man had been working there for years, yet no one understood or knew what the man was doing.

As the conversations continued over time, the townspeople determined the man was being paid too much to do something obviously not important or needed. Everyone agreed to fire the man at the top of the hill.

However, after firing the man, it didn't take long before everyone in town knew what work the man had been doing, because the entire town flooded. You see, no one knew the work the man was performing upstream was helping and protecting the townspeople downstream. I am sure everyone in town at that point was thinking if we knew then what we know now, we wouldn't have fired the man who worked at the top of the hill.

In the bible, Peter denied Jesus three times. No doubt about it, if Peter had it to do all over again, he would surely say, "If I knew then what I know now."

Moses, after killing the Egyptian would say, "If I knew then what I know now."

David would have said after sending Bathsheba's husband to the front line of battle, "If I knew then what I know now."

Sometimes, when we are in a bad situation, we find ourselves thinking, if I knew then what I know now. Many of us can think back to the point in our lives that we surrendered our lives to the Lord. After salvation, regardless of what we thought we knew, we realized we did not have the peace of knowing Jesus in the pardoning of our sins.

When you come into the family of the Lord, you will have peace and joy that the world cannot take away. If you thought you were happy before salvation, you will be overflowing with joy after salvation.

As a child of the King of Kings and Lord of Lords, you can truly say if I knew then what I know now, I would have come to Jesus years ago. Be blessed as you read *I Thought I Knew.*

This poem is dedicated to Bishop Wilfret Johnson, strong soldier in the army of the Most-High God. My brother, we are waiting for *'Upstream Downstream, Part II.'*

I Thought I Knew

In years gone by
I always thought I knew
How wonderful God's love was
for me and for you

I thought I knew how and why
it had all begun
I thought I knew because
of the great sacrifice His son

I thought I knew
how much God cared for me
As evidenced by the blood
He shed for me on Calvary

I thought about the sun, the moon
and the stars above
but I had only a glimpse
of His works and His magnificent love

One day with tears in my eyes
and a heart that was shattered
I looked for the Savior
Nothing else mattered

I looked for His comfort
to ease my pain
I knew that without Him
everlasting life I would not gain

My spirit was reaching
for that inner peace
And that can only come
through a total release

The night the Holy Spirit
moved on the inside of me
My whole life changed
a difference I could even see

Now I'm taught and led
by the Holy Spirit each day
As a new creature in Christ
I'm changed in a blessed way

I'm a baby on milk
sucking up the word
Praying for the strength
to live what I've heard

Day by day
I'm growing stronger
I'm glad because Jesus is coming back
it won't be much longer.

Acts 16:27-31 (King James Version)

[27] And the keeper of the prison awaking out of his sleep, and seeing the prison doors open, he drew out his sword, and would have killed himself, supposing that the prisoners had been fled.
[28] But Paul cried with a loud voice, saying, Do thyself no harm: for we are all here.
[29] Then he called for a light, and sprang in, and came trembling, and fell down before Paul and Silas,
[30] And brought them out, and said, Sirs, what must I do to be saved?
[31] And they said, Believe on the Lord Jesus Christ, and thou shalt be saved, and thy house.

My Inspiration for: If You Really

I was driving from San Juan, Puerto Rico to my condo in Fajardo, Puerto Rico and the traffic was heavy. I was sure it would be at least two hours or more before I reached home. As I sat in traffic, not moving, I began to think about the new home the Lord was blessing me with in North Carolina. I thought about how God had recently opened the floodgates of heaven and poured out so many blessings in my life. I thanked God because His good measure truly had been pressed down, shaken together, and was running over.

I thought, truly there is no way to explain it in the 'natural.' At that moment, God spoke into my spirit and said, "How will you answer, when asked, 'where do your blessings come from?'" Truly God, you are my Jehovah Jireh, my provider. God, you said you would supply "all of my need" according to your richest in glory by Christ Jesus. God, you said if I trust in You and do good, I would be fed. You said if I delight myself also in You; that You would give me the desires of my heart. Oh, God of Abraham, Isaac, and Jacob, Lord I praise Your name for truly Your blessings have overtaken me. Let the Lord of hosts bless you as you read, *If You Really*.

This poem is dedicated to Lott Carey Foreign Mission Convention and missionaries all over the world. You open your hearts and show the love and blessings of our Lord and Savior Jesus the Christ to the world.

If You Really

If you really want to know
where my blessings come from
I'll just lift my hands in praise
and say God's only begotten son

If you really want to know
how to be closer to God's love
I'll just lift my hands in praise
and tell you to set your affections
on things above

If you really want to know
Why I don't mind
when people do me wrong
I'll just lift my hands in praise
and say it is to Jesus that I belong

If you really want to know
why I have a smile on my face
I'll just lift my hands in praise and say
it is God's love
and His amazing grace!

Deuteronomy 28:2 (King James Version)
And all these blessings shall come on thee,
and overtake thee, if thou shalt hearken unto
the voice of the LORD thy God.

My Inspiration for: Leading with Love

Nehemiah is the ultimate example of leadership. As a former civilian working for the United States Navy, I was blessed with many leadership opportunities. I participated in many training and leadership classes; however, my greatest example of true leadership is found in the book of Nehemiah.

When Nehemiah heard the news that his people were in trouble, he went to the king and asked for permission to leave so he could help them. Upon arriving at his destination, Nehemiah, quietly and prayerfully went out at night to assess the situation. After doing so, Nehemiah called the people together to do a work for the Lord. He did not focus on what skills the people had, nor the sad state of the materials he had to use.

Nehemiah only focused on the work God needed them to do. I call that a faith experience.

After organizing the people and establishing a plan for the rebuilding efforts, Nehemiah had what I call a commitment experience. Nehemiah would not stop moving forward to accomplish his appointed task. He could not be frightened, he could not be enticed, he could not be lured, nor could he be discouraged. I call that a steadfast experience.

Today, there are Nehemiah's in our midst. Sometimes you might meet him at church, at work, at a gas station, at a sporting event, or even standing in line at a grocery store. Late one night, I met Nehemiah in the lobby of a hotel.

It was after one of the evening sessions of the General Baptist State Convention of North Carolina. I shared a room with two other ladies and we had managed to do everything that evening except have dinner. At about 10:00 o'clock that evening, I was tasked to pick up our delivery order from a nearby restaurant in the downstairs lobby.

Because it was late at night, and I was only to be downstairs for a few minutes to pick up the delivery order, I didn't bother to change from my 'in the room clothes.' So, with a bandana on my head, a faded tee shirt, and what we in North Carolina call 'knee knockers' and flip flops, I made my way down to the lobby. I stood at the desk and waited. Forty-five minutes passed and no food. One hour and three phone calls later, still no food. My roommates were begging me to wait for the order, because they were starving, and so was I. It was now almost midnight and – you guessed it – no food.

I heard voices and saw several association members, one of which I instantly recognized. Of course they saw me, because there was nowhere to hide. I was truly embarrassed. We exchanged greetings and the gentleman I recognized asked me what was I doing in the lobby by myself so late at night. Because of my appearance, he probably thought I was accidently locked out of my room. I told him I was waiting for our food to be delivered. He asked how long I had been waiting and I responded, "about two hours." He said, "don't wait any longer, we have plenty of food in our suite; we are on the way out; just go up to the suite and tell them I sent you."

I graciously thanked him and watched them walk away. He must have read my thoughts … 'no way am I going to someone's suite looking like this' … because he stopped and turned around. Seeing I had not moved, he came back and said, "come on, I will walk you up to the suite."

So, Nehemiah the leader, Nehemiah the caring and compassion man of God, Nehemiah the anointed servant stopped to help someone he didn't know. I call him Nehemiah, but the one that stopped that night was the Dr. Gregory Moss, Sr., who at that time was the newly elected President of the General Baptist State Convention of North Carolina (a membership of 1,600 churches) and pastor of St. Paul's Missionary Baptist Church, Charlotte, North Carolina (under his leadership, the church grew by more than 3,500 members to over 5,000 members, of which more than half had come by baptism).

Dr. Moss would also later be elected and serve as the national president of the Lott Carey Foreign Mission Convention, which partners with indigenous communities and leaders around the world.

To the least of them, let us receive them with the love Christ Jesus placed in our hearts. May the peace of God rule in our hearts. I pray you are blessed as you read *Leading with Love.*

The poem is dedicated to my friend and brother in Christ, Dr. Gregory Moss, Sr. My brother; you said, "I understand the difference between authority and power." Yes, you do; you built trusted relationships; the hurting, the hungry, the broken, and the lost filled the house and heard the message of salvation.

Bless you for your tireless quest to spread the gospel inside and outside the walls.

Leading with Love

I am the leader
Who is leading with love
The agape kind
From the Father above
When you lead with love
You have a different approach
You realize it's your responsibility
To encourage and coach

Leading by example
Instead of do as I say
With the Holy Spirit leading
And guiding you along the way
I ask and not demand
For a job to be done
Laboring in love
The obstacles are easily overcome

Your errors I won't discuss
In idle conversation
I'll teach you so we can benefit
From your full participation
I cannot be you
Nor can you be me
But we are called to be a light
For the world to see

For God is love
And Jesus gave us a command
As he loved us
We are to love our fellow man
Oh, it's easy to say that we love
Our sister and our brother
But it's hard to see by the way
We sometimes treat each other

I've learned that it's not what you can give
But what you can take
I've learned that it's so easy
To magnify someone else's mistakes
I've learned to look at you
Through eyes of love
I've learned not to focus on me or you
But the Father above

I cover your transgressions
And put them in the past
I hold fast to love because
It's the only thing that will last.

Nehemiah 2:18 (King James Version)
Then I told them of the hand of my God which
was good upon me; as also the king's words
that he had spoken unto me. And they said,
let us rise up and build. So, they strengthened
their hands for this good work.

My Inspiration for: My Greatest Love

I had no idea how special the day would be for Barbara that bright, sunny day I walked into her office. However, the moment I saw tears streaming down her face, I knew that Barbara was a broken woman. In my heart, I realized Barbara was having a 'Leah experience' and she was feeling unloved, unwanted, and unappreciated. When you have been there yourself, it is easy to read the signs of an aching heart, shattered dreams, and broken promises.

Over several years, I had the occasion to share many things with Barbara, but today, I knew the Lord was knocking on the door of her heart. It was her appointed time to respond to the Lord's call. Barbara needed true love. Barbara needed a love that would stand the test of time. Barbara needed unconditional love. Barbara needed the love that only our Lord and Savior Jesus Christ can give.

I began to share the love of our Lord and Savior, Jesus Christ, and the resurrection power of His blood, Barbara began to cry. I spoke with Barbara of an old rugged cross, an early morning rising, and Jesus ascending into heaven to sit on the right hand of God.

Barbara began to say in between sobbing, "I have been in a relationship with someone outside of the bonds of matrimony for 25 years. Even now, I am not sure I can break the ties." Barbara looked at me and asked why would Jesus save me? I simply responded, because He loves you, Barbara. Jesus is waiting with open arms. It is never too late to receive the gift of salvation.

The Bible says to come as you are and let the power of the blood shed by Jesus cleanse you from all unrighteousness. I told Barbara to come as the woman with her back bent with a spirit of infirmity for 18 years.

Come as the woman of Samaria who went to the well in the heat of the day. Come as the woman with the issue of blood for 12 years who touched the hem of His garment. Come as the beloved in the Lord and receive salvation by the Lord's grace and mercy. That day Barbara gave her life to the Lord. As we embraced and cried tears of joy, I told her you have given your life to the Lord; you are now a new creature in Christ.

Later that night, I began to think of who I was before I was saved by the blood of the Lamb. As I thought about how far God had brought me. I began to thank Him for giving me the opportunity to lead another soul to Him. Oh, love, sweet love, my greatest love ... Barbara had now quenched her thirst with water from the well of life.

This poem is dedicated to every woman that has felt or feels unloved or unwanted or unappreciated. I invite you to come, taste, and see that the Lord IS good. He will be your greatest love.

My Greatest Love

When I look back over my life
And what I've been through
I realize that what has kept me
Was the love of Jesus so sweet and so true

I haven't always been
What God called me to be
Yet, I knew in my heart
That He still loved me

Sometimes it wasn't easy
When people judged me
And said that I didn't measure up
They told me I wasn't even worthy
To drink from God's Holy cup

But I cried out in a loud voice
Like the man who was blind
I held on to grace
And remembered that mercy was still mine

I said Jesus I've been searching
And never finding what's missing in my life
I'm tired of the pain
the loneliness and the strife

I'm tired of wearing a smile
To cover the pain that I feel inside
I'm so ashamed of my life
But I know I can no longer hide

God reached out
And gently took my hand
And begin to share the gospel
And His redemption plan

God said it is my desire
That all will come and receive
All you need my child
Is the faith to believe

I listened to the plan of salvation
As my eyes filled with tears
Because I realized that is what
I had been longing for so many years

Praise God that I received Jesus
As my Lord and Savior that day
Now I am depending on Him
To lead me and show me the way

I am a new creature in Christ
And began life anew
Now I have my greatest love
And that love Jesus is You!

Isaiah 54:4-8 (King James Version)
[4] Fear not; for thou shalt not be ashamed: neither be thou confounded; for thou shalt not be put to shame: for thou shalt forget the shame of thy youth, and shalt not remember the reproach of thy widowhood any more.
[5] For thy Maker is thine husband; the Lord of hosts is his name; and thy Redeemer the Holy One of Israel; The God of the whole earth shall he be called.
[6] For the Lord hath called thee as a woman forsaken and grieved in spirit, and a wife of youth, when thou wast refused, saith thy God.
[7] For a small moment have I forsaken thee; but with great mercies will I gather thee.
[8] In a little wrath I hid my face from thee for a moment; but with everlasting kindness will I have mercy on thee, saith the Lord thy Redeemer.

My Inspiration for: New Orleans

I received the call from my godmother about a New Orleans family in need of assistance in New Bern, North Carolina. The family was like many whom had been displaced because of hurricane Katrina. The first question that came to my mind was … certainly the family had received assistance from many local organizations and churches by now? My godmother assured me although people had visited them, no one had provided any assistance. My godmother gave me a telephone number to contact the family, and I promised to call. When I called, I was told the family did not need clothing, but food and money to get their lives restarted. I also was informed the family had contacted many local agencies, but none of the organizations were able to offer any assistance.

At the time of the hurricane, Reverend Earl was 68 years and Ms. Rose was 65. Both had been receiving social security in New Orleans. Of course, I asked if the couple had contacted the local Social Security office to request that their checks be issued in North Carolina. Ms. Rose explained a government representative at the Social Security office told them if they tried to collect checks in North Carolina they would face criminal charges.

This was just one of the many glitches in the system unresolved by the government who seemed to be stymied with the disaster and the massive number of hurricane victims.

Fortunately, after several days, clarification to the Social Security enabled the family to file for benefits in North Carolina and receive their benefits.

I asked Reverend Earl if they had received assistance from local churches and civic organizations. Reverend Earl stated that he and his family were featured in a local news article with several people from community and church groups. However, his family never received assistance from them.

One obstacle to receiving assistance –
after the churches collected the money – they
were not sure how to divide and distribute the
money without knowing the number of families
that were in need. They wanted to determine
how many families had relocated to New Bern
as a result of Hurricane Katrina before the
disbursing funds. The challenge was how to
collect that information. Unfortunately, this
challenge left many needy families temporarily
without any assistance.

When I checked the computer to verify
Reverend Earl and Ms. Rose as hurricane
victims, I saw their names and that they had
indeed had been in several shelters. I also
read an article about Reverend Earl and it
spoke of him as the Assistant Pastor of a
Baptist church in New Orleans. It was so sad
to think of people their age having to make
such a long pilgrimage to my hometown and
heart-crushing to find these victims were
getting so many doors slammed in their faces.

Little did I realize just how much
Reverend Earl and Ms. Rose had endured
and suffered to get from New Orleans to North
Carolina. I traveled to New Bern with another
sister in the Lord to provide money and food I

had collected from friends and dinners sold at the church; but I was not prepared for what I encountered.

When we arrived at the home where Reverend Earl and Ms. Rose were staying, he saw us and ran out to meet us and to help us with the packages. Before doing anything else, Reverend Earl asked us to join hands, and he began to pray for us. In spite of all they had endured, his prayers were not for him and his family, *but for us.* He prayed God would bless us for our kindness and love. As I stood in the small circle of prayer, I began to cry uncontrollably. Reverend Earl thanked us and said it was the first time since arriving to New Bern that money had been put into his hands. He was so appreciative of the food and gave thanks to God for sending angels of mercy.

I cried for Reverend Earl and Ms. Rose, I cried for their families, I cried for the families I did not know, and I think most of all I cried, because I was grateful God had called me to be a blessing. I was grateful I had listened to the small voice inside me.

Only from God's view would it make sense that I would be a chosen vessel to travel three hours to provide comfort and assistance to this awesome man of God and his family. It was truly an awesome blessing. Thank you Jesus!

After the prayer, Reverend Earl told us their story. They had remained in New Orleans simply because they were not anticipating the worse, and because they had a two-story home with an attic. It was only after the weather turned worse, they realized what they thought would be a safe-haven would not be enough. To escape, they had to break through the attic and climb out on the roof. After three days, one of their sons escaped from his own rooftop to help them.

Reverend Earl and Ms. Rose were determined to survive and had to jump from the roof into the water. Ms. Rose made it to the boat, but Reverend Earl landed in water and was almost lost in the current. God stepped in and enabled his son to rescue him.

Reverend Earl and Ms. Rose made their way from New Orleans, staying in three separate shelters, before leaving Louisiana.

While at the last shelter, God sent an angel in the form of a Catholic Priest who gave them airline tickets to North Carolina, luggage, clothing, and a ride to the airport.

Reverend Earl stated through the ordeal that he never lost faith in God. Reverend Earl and Ms. Rose are just two people who survived Katrina; but their story and their trials and struggles are too familiar. Today they are settled, established in a home of their own and doing very well. I have not spoken with them in several years. I do know one thing.

Where ever Reverend Earl and Ms. Rose are, they are blessing others. Blessed be the name of the Lord.

This poem is dedicated to Reverend Earl and Ms. Rose and the hurricane Katrina victims and their families. It is also dedicated to spirit, faith, and determination of my brothers and sisters in Louisiana.

New Orleans

Today many are asking
Why did the levees break
What was God doing
To allow so much heartache

What about the old people, the innocent
babies
And the saints calling on His name
Why didn't help come in time
Why are we now a nation in shame

The city officials looking to the state
The state looking to the nation
Mass confusion, death and destruction
God where are you
We need your help in this situation

They say you opened the flood gates
And let your fury roar
The city of fun and music
Now has piles of debris washed up on the
shore

All the people that suffered
It was truly sad
The chaos and the riots
It seemed the whole world had gone mad

I don't know why it happened
But You said all things work together for good
I know You will come to the rescue
Just like You promised You would

When I felt all hope was gone
I looked up in the sky
I saw You looking down on me
With a tear in Your eye

Oh, God, I praise You for
Your love and righteousness
I bless Your name for who You are to me
Because of faith I don't need to understand
I trust You though the end I may not see

Forgive me for doubting
I know that there is nothing impossible for
You to do
I praise your name oh Lord
And thank you for mercies anew

You promised us joy in the morning
You said I will restore you and remove your
pain
You said let not your heart be troubled
All your trials are stored up for eternal gain

In the beauty of Your holiness
With Jesus sitting on Your right side
You lovingly whispered to us
In your hearts let My words abide

Remember that what I blessed you with
No one can take away
Rejoice and get ready to receive
A mighty move of My power and blessings are
on the way!

Philippians 4:13 (King James Version)
I can do all things through Christ which
strengthens me.

My Inspiration for: On My Way

Sitting at my sales booth of African arts and clothing, I looked around and there was absolutely no one moving about. It was the kind of quietness that was certainly abnormal for a Saturday on a large military base. As I was looking through my bag, hoping I had remembered to bring my Bible, I saw a paper with a scripture. I had printed it earlier and it said, "Speak Lord for your servant heareth."

This was my word for today. As I slowly read the scripture from Psalms 18:33, David declared the Lord would make his feet as hinds' feet. God also proclaimed it in 2 Samuel 22:34. The prophet Habakkuk declared, 'The LORD God is my strength, and he will make my feet like hinds' feet, and he will make me to walk upon mine high places.'

I so love the way the Lord uses examples to make sure we understand His word. I would have never imagined just thinking about a deer would bring tears to my eyes, but it did. You see a hind is a female red deer whose home is in the mountains. Every motion of the hind is followed through with a single-focused consistency, making it the most sure-footed of all mountain animals. You see the hind is known for its ability to climb mountains. However, the most unique thing is that when the hind walks and climbs the hind feet will go perfectly into the foot prints left by the front feet. Therefore, the hind only leaves one set of foots prints.

So, the Lord is speaking to us in this scripture ... follow in my steps. I thought how wonderful it is that, like the deer, all we need to do is to follow in the steps that Jesus has taken, and one day He promised us that we will see Him face-to-face. Praise God for hinds' feet and praise God for Jesus. Be blessed as you read On My Way.

This poem is dedicated to the men and women of our armed services who stand the watch all over the world and our veterans whom we shall forever remember and cherish.

On My Way

He girdeth me with strength
And makes perfect my way
It is my God of miracles
That blesses me each and every day

Blessings overtake me
I'm blessed going out and coming in
As I face the challenges of life
Through Jesus the battles I will win

He maketh my feet like hind's feet
With confidence, I follow my master
I smile as I remember
The oil in the box of alabaster

No need for me to worry
About what tomorrow will bring
Because I have a hedge of protection
Set in place by Jesus my king

If I follow where He leads me
Holding His hand as I run the race
In the end, I will get my crown
And find rest in a heavenly place.

2 Samuel 22:34 (King James Version)
He maketh my feet like hinds' feet: and setteth
me upon my high places.

Psalm 18:33 (King James Version)
He maketh my feet like hinds' feet, and setteth
me upon my high places.

Habakkuk 3:19 (King James Version)
The LORD God is my strength, and he will
make my feet like hinds' feet, and he will
make me to walk upon mine high places. To
the chief singer on my stringed instruments.

My Inspiration for: One More Time

As a child growing up in North Carolina, I remember being in church and hearing old folks give their testimonies. Many times, they would start out so quietly you would have to strain to hear them, but after a little while they would throw their hands in the air, cry, and speak so loudly you needed to cover your ears. Regardless of how quietly they started, everyone always knew what was coming next.

There were some things you were so accustomed to hearing in my church, when you heard the first few words, you could always fill in the blanks. For example, when you heard the Lord has brought me … you knew the rest was a mighty long way. He is my bright and … morning star; He is the lily of … the valley; He is a doctor … in the sick room, a lawyer … in the court room, a friend to … the friendless; I thank the Lord for

a reasonable portion … of health and
strength; I am thankful that I woke up with the
activity … of my limbs; I am glad to be in the
house of the Lord … one more time; it is me,
Lord, standing in … the need of prayer; he
woke me up this morning and … started me
on my way; Lord you have been a bridge …
over troubled water; and I am thankful for just
one more day, a day … that I've never seen
before.

What was sometimes funny and routine
as a child has become special and precious
as the years have passed. Truly I know what
the old saints meant when they prayed, Lord I
am thankful for just one more day. Be blessed
as you read *One More Time.*

This poem is dedicated to senior saints
all over the world. For truly God is not
unrighteous to forget your labor of love. It shall
be well with thee.

One More Time

When I was a young girl
I used to hear old people pray Lord,
I am so thankful
For just one more day

Now that the years have passed
I understand the mystery and the surprise
I see the beauty of God's gift
In each sunset and each sunrise

I see it's one more time to get it right
As I witness to young and old
I see it's one more time to praise the one
Who is the keeper of my soul

I see it's one more time
To see the clouds, hear the birds
And great someone with a holy kiss
I see it's one more time to thank God
For an opportunity not missed!

Colossians 3:14-15 (King James Version)
And above all these things put on charity,
which is the bond of perfectness. And let the
peace of God rule in your hearts, to the which
also ye are called in one body; and be ye
thankful.

My Inspiration for: Thank You Jesus

Years ago, I heard the late Reverend Otis Turnage, of Mt. Zion Holiness Church in New Bern, North Carolina, preach about having the word in our head, our heart, and our hand. For years, I had the word in my hand and my head. I could easily open the bible and quickly find scriptures to read. As time passed, I was also able to remember many of the scriptures.

What was missing was the power of having the word in my heart. So, are you wondering what is the difference? The difference is that God is all about the heart. The bible says that the Lord search the heart and try the reins, to give every man according to his ways, and according to the fruit of his doings. The Lord does not search our hands or our minds only our hearts. It is having the word hidden in our heart that gives us power to walk without fainting. It is having the word hidden in our heart that lets us conquer instead of being conquered. It is having the word hidden in our heart that lets us love and not hate our enemies.

It is with a grateful heart I shall never forget what Jesus did for me. It is with a grateful heart I shall never forget how He set me free. It is with a grateful heart I will always remember to thank the Lord for saving me.

For me, He suffered, bled, died, and rose from the dead, that I might have a chance for eternal life.

This poem is dedicated all those who one day almost laid down in defeat, but thanks to Him who is able to keep us from falling rose up in victory.

Thank You Jesus

Thank you Jesus
for doing a new work in me
Thank you Jesus for the fire
burning so bright in me

When I first met You
I knew at a glance
That without You in my life
I didn't stand a chance

Over the rough roads of life
and down the valley of despair
No hope left
and no one to care

On pillows soaked with tears
and a heart that was broken
When I heard your sweet voice Jesus
I knew You had spoken

The world offered its best
but I was still full of pain
And satan had me bound
with the strongest chain

But in a brief moment
You touched my wounded heart
And I found myself saying
"Satan from me you must depart"

You started working
on filling me up with Your love
Then You told me to
set my affections on things above

You told me You had
prepared a place for me
You said in My name
from satan you are forever free

You told me of the victory
and the blood that You shed for me
Oh, thank you Jesus
for the new life You have given me

You placed in my heart
my head and my hand
The message of salvation
for the unsaved man

And just when I thought
Your work was complete
You told me how to bring
the enemy down in defeat

I started out a sinner
with no hope in sight
When I looked again Jesus
I was on the battlefield to fight

In one hand was the sword of the spirit
the precious word of God
I looked at my feet
they were now Holy Ghost shod

I had the shield of faith
and the helmet of salvation on my head
Oh, thank you Jesus that over the enemy
I have the power to tread

Jesus, how can I thank You
for opening my blind eyes to see
Oh I know, I can live
so that others can see You in me.

Ephesians 6:12-13 (King James Version)
For we wrestle not against flesh and blood,
but against principalities, against powers,
against the rulers of the darkness of this
world, against spiritual wickedness in high
places. Wherefore take unto you the whole
armor of God, that ye may be able to
withstand in the evil day, and having done all,
to stand.

My Inspiration for: The Invitation

Imagine an invitation to an event of a lifetime to continuously enjoy peace, love, joy, and protection. You can accept the invitation and instantly become a member of the royal family. Your father is standing by with outstretched arms waiting to welcome you. As you turn around, you see two special friends named 'Grace' and 'Mercy.' Think of the gold engraved invitation:

"You are cordially invited to sup with me and I with you. I want to love you and give you an eternal resting place where every day will be Sunday. Now before you ask, you didn't earn the right to this invitation. You see, I loved you so much I gave my only begotten son who shed his blood for you.

Please don't delay in responding to this invitation, because no one knows the day or the hour when my Son shall reappear."

This poem is dedicated to the lonely, the lost, the hurting and the broken. Jesus is waiting on you!

The Invitation

Whether you're rich
or whether you're poor
I pray that you'll answer
when Jesus knocks at your door

Jesus is the only rock
on which you can stand
He even told us
place your confidence in no man

It doesn't matter
if you are young or old
Jesus is the best story
you'll ever be told

He is so sweet
and his goodness is everlasting
Oh, what a joy
to give yourself to prayer and fasting

In the midnight hour
when you don't have a friend
Just try calling on Jesus
He'll be with you to the end

People may dig up
all the wrong that you've done
But just walk in the path
of God's only begotten Son

Jesus has already prayed
that your faith would not fail
He can deliver you
from alcohol, drugs, even jail

Just call on His name
and Jesus will be yours today
He wants you for his child
to lead you and show you the way

It will be joy in morning
and joy at night
And one day you'll be bound
for that heavenly flight

If you start to doubt Him
just think of the empty grave
I know for myself
that only Jesus has the power to save

You can be washed in His blood
and be born again
You'll be clean and whole
no longer in a life of sin

Come as you are
let Him be your lord and your king
Jesus is waiting for your hand
He wants to give you a heavenly ring

You will now be strong
even when you are weak
Be still and be quiet
Jesus is about to speak.

Romans 10:9 (King James Version)
That if thou shalt confess with thy mouth the
Lord Jesus, and shalt believe in thine heart
that God hath raised him from the dead, thou
shalt be saved.

My Inspiration for:
The Prayer of the Perfect Christian

I was on my way to church one Sunday when suddenly, I heard a loud noise coming from the rear of my car. I pulled over quickly and stepped out of the car. I saw my left rear tire had blown and was completely flat. I stood there praying, asking the Lord to come to my rescue. I was alone, and did not know how to change a tire, nor did I have a cell phone to call for help.

As I stood there praying, I looked up just in time to see one of the deacons from my church and his family approaching on their way to morning service. They looked at me and I looked at them. In disbelief, I watched as they quickly drove right past me. Ok. I said the devil is a liar and I will not let him steal my joy.

Seconds later, I saw one of our choir members approaching. Again, he looked at me and I looked at him, but this time I was dumbfounded as he also quickly kept going right past my disabled car.

At this point, I am talking to the Lord. Lord, you know I am here alone. You said in your word, two are better than one, because they have a better reward for their labor but woe to the one that is alone because if he falls there is no one to pick him up. Lord, you know that I am a widow and a widow indeed. You promised you would be my company keeper and my provider.

At this point, the unexpected happened. A police car stopped, but instead of offering to help me, they were getting ready to write me a ticket. Apparently, I was parked in the wrong place. Ok. This was not going to end nicely.

I opened my mouth in praise and prayer and told those young men I was on my way to church. I said I could not help but stop because my rear tire blew out. I needed someone to help me fix my tire or I needed a ride to church.

Well, you know God can put the heart of the king in your hands. That said, he put the heart of those young officers in my hands, because they assisted me in getting my tire changed and did not give me a ticket.

Remember the deacon and the choir member? I was later told that both of them mentioned to several people in the congregation they saw me on the side of the road. But, they neglected to share they had passed me by, leaving me there alone.

After this experience, I began to think about 'religious folks' that 'major' in tradition and 'minor' in relationship with Jesus. Oh, the perfect Christian, they are truly busy in their own perfection, while they diligently check off the boxes in preparation for their heaven-bound experience. They also have to devote time to get the beam out of the eyes of others. They feel compelled to share the sermon that brings correction to the lives of others. They are very quick to pray for the faults of others. As model Christians, they must stay up on their pedestal, less they rub elbows with those who have not arrived to their level of Christian level of perfection.

These folks are so 'religious' and upright they delight in correcting the preacher, training the deacons, coaching the trustees, directing the missionaries, expounding on the Bible study lessons, bringing reformation to the

Sunday school class, and of course, giving the Lord some tips on how to handle folks who are not meeting the 'Christian' standards.

Mercy me! They are so busy I wonder if they will have time to make it to Heaven. This poem is dedicated to *Perfect Christians* all over the world.

The Prayer of the Perfect Christian

Jesus, you won't believe
what happened to me today
I was minding my own business
In my everyday Christian way

When out of nowhere
Came this old drunk
He was so dirty
He smelled worse than a skunk

I pinched my nose
To block out the smell
But he had the nerve to speak to me
And say I'm doing very well

Can you believe
he stopped to talk to me
Doesn't he know I'm your child
A light for the world to see

Every day they come
The drunks, the needy, and the poor
I can't believe they keep coming
As many times as I've slammed my door

So, Jesus, this is my prayer
and please put it in first place
You see I'm so sick and tired
Of this whole human race

I want more
good upstanding Christians like myself
Ones who are not begging
But have some financial wealth

Jesus, please remove from my path
Those who can hardly read and write
When I have to be around them
I can't help notice they're really not too bright

How can they do
What they can't possible understand
It's the ignorant folks I'm talking about
The ones who can't even spell command

I'll be so glad
When I get up to heaven with you
Away from all these folks
Who make me feel like beating them black
and blue

Jesus, I hope you didn't miss
Good old cousin Sally
That was last Saturday night
She got drunk and fell down in the alley

She's no good
And will never cause you anything but a frown
Guess everybody knows
She's slept with almost every man in town

Now Jesus, it's those types of people
I'm talking about
But I don't want to forget those crazy ones
That do the Holy Ghost shout

I tell you they're always carrying on such a
ruckus and a fuss
If I weren't on my way to heaven
It would be enough to make me cuss

You see what I have to live with
And this is all the time
The drunks, the crazies
And the ones begging for a dime

It seems that every time
I'm on my way to church for worship and
praise
Someone has the nerve to ask for my help
These nuts must be in a daze

Oh, for the day
That I'll get my reward from you
It's got to be a lot
With all that I've been through

I won't hold You
Cause these folks need a lot of working on
Jesus? ... Jesus? ... Hmm
I think He's gone!

Luke 18:9-14 (King James Version)
[9] And he spake this parable unto certain which trusted in themselves that they were righteous, and despised others:
[10] Two men went up into the temple to pray; the one a Pharisee, and the other a publican.
[11] The Pharisee stood and prayed thus with himself, God, I thank thee, that I am not as other men are, extortioners, unjust, adulterers, or even as this publican.
[12] I fast twice in the week, I give tithes of all that I possess.
[13] And the publican, standing afar off, would not lift up so much as his eyes unto heaven, but smote upon his breast, saying, God be merciful to me a sinner.
[14] I tell you, this man went down to his house justified rather than the other: for every one that exalteth himself shall be abased; and he that humbleth himself shall be exalted.

My Inspiration for: The Ring on My Hand

For years, I was a very religious person. I had been in church all my life and knew all the Bible stories. But, something happened in my life that caused me to crumble emotionally. The once happy and outgoing person I was disappeared. I became a sad, sobbing recluse. This happened when I lost my earthly father whom I loved, cherished, and adored. I had been a daddy's girl all my life.

I remember the story my mother used to tell me. She said when I was a baby every day at just at about the time my daddy would come home for lunch or at the end of the work day, I would crawl over to the door and start looking out. Even though I could not tell time, something triggered inside of me and I knew when to go to the door to watch for my daddy.

Over the years my daddy was my friend, my defender, the one I would talk to about my problems and the one who always made me feel better by just smiling and saying, "It will be all right little girl." The fact I was a grown woman didn't matter. I was still daddy's little girl. Oh, how I loved my daddy. When my daddy passed, it seemed my whole world had collapsed. I was always strong, but I became weak, helpless, and hopeless.

In the middle of my sorrow, it seemed my heart was so broken I thought I would never stop hurting. However, something happened at the lowest point of my life. I found a true relationship with the Lord. I found comfort in His word and His truth became my shield and protection. I found hope in His promises. I found joy even in my sorrow. I found love and peace. Yes, I found a friend and a comforter. Jesus gave me a ring … a most beautiful ring. He has one for you too.

Read and be blessed as you read *The Ring on My Hand*.

This poem is dedicated to all those that are out there feeling that you've done too much, that you've gone too far, that you're down too low to come home … Jesus is waiting and he has a ring just for you.

The Ring on My Hand

The ring on my hand
Is something to see
I was given by God's grace
And was nothing done by me

I was lost and alone
An enemy of God
With the gospel of peace
My feet were not shod

With tender, loving mercy
And love from His Son
He spoke to my heart
And told me the race could be won

I thought about my life
How empty and sad
But when I thought about Jesus
I became exceedingly glad

I remembered He laid down His life
So that I might live
God loved me so much
He gave the best that He had to give

The pain that He suffered
On Calvary that day
Let the world know He is the light
The truth and the way

The riches He offered
To even a sinner like me
The price of salvation
No charge, it's free

He is my rock
On Him I depend
No matter the battle
Jesus can defend

When He went to the Father
He didn't leave me alone
The comforter, the Holy Spirit
Now makes me His home

The ring on my hand
Is something to see
It was given by God's grace
And was nothing done by me

Eight jewels are on
My beautiful ring
Given to me by Jesus
The King of Kings

Peace, hope, patience
Are three of the stones
I'm so glad I'm flesh of His flesh
And bone of His bones

Access by faith
Experience and love
Three more of God's blessings
From above

Glory in tribulation
And joy are the last of the eight
Thank God for my salvation
And the fact that I didn't wait too late!

Luke 15:20-22 (King James Version)
[20] And he arose, and came to his father. But when he was yet a great way off, his father saw him, and had compassion, and ran, and fell on his neck, and kissed him.
[21] And the son said unto him, Father, I have sinned against heaven, and in thy sight, and am no more worthy to be called thy son.
[22] But the father said to his servants, Bring forth the best robe, and put it on him; and put a ring on his hand, and shoes on his feet:

My Inspiration for: Until We Meet Again

As believers, we have assurance we will one day see our loved ones whom have gone on to be with the Lord. However, it is still hard when they pass from earth to glory. We miss being with them. We miss talking to them. We miss seeing their smiles. We miss quiet times when absolutely nothing was said yet everything was said. We miss laughs, vacations, and family dinners. We miss sharing holidays, anniversaries, birthdays, and those special moments together. We miss warm touches, embraces, hugs of comfort, and healing kisses to make it all better.

Having to live with the loss of a loved one is like having a hole in our heart. After a while we can smile in loving remembrance of the love shared and reflect on precious memories that will last forever. Be blessed as you read *Until We Meet Again*.

This poem is dedicated to the memory of Mildred Hill and Essie Lee Hill McMillian grandmother and mother of Glendell Hill and great grandmother and grandmother of Donna Hill Brandveen.

Until We Meet Again

My spirit is free
And God knows that I did my best
The battle has been won
And now I am at rest

My home is now heaven
And with the angels I am singing
Safely in the arms of Jesus
Around the throne I am clinging

To God be the glory
For the place He prepared for me
It is even more beautiful
Than I ever thought it would be

It was a hard journey
But I said I won't complain
Because all my trials were treasure
Stored up for eternal gain

Never forget the smiles, the love
And the joy that we shared
And never forget
How much I cared!

Revelation 21:4 (King James Version)
And God shall wipe away all tears from their
eyes; and there shall be no more death,
neither sorrow, nor crying, neither shall there
be any more pain: for the former things are
passed away.

My Inspiration for: You Are

I sat on my balcony in Puerto Rico at 4:30 o'clock in the morning. It was quiet, except for the sound of the water splashing against the rocks. It was peaceful and I was praying and thanking God for just being God. I thought about my life and how God had brought me over the rough roads and dried my tears. I started to think about how He had provided for me. I thought about how He had healed me.

At that point, I thought about the fact God is so many things to me and I began to pray 'thank you' to The Lord, Most High, The Lord, The Everlasting God, The God Who is Sufficient for the Needs of His People, The Eternal Creator, The Lord our Provider, The Lord our Banner, The Lord our Healer, The Lord our Peace, The Lord our Righteousness, The Lord our Sanctifier, The Lord of Hosts,

The Lord is Present, The Lord our Shepherd,
The Lord our Maker, and The Lord our God.

You are ... You are ... You are ...

This poem is dedicated to those who teach the word of God with wisdom and knowledge. They teach with a burden to share the gospel in such a way that ordinary people will gain an understanding of the bible. They teach because their love of God compels them to lovingly share the gospel that Christ Jesus is our Lord and our Savior.

Special love to Bishop Jessie Williams, Reverend Larry Ponds, Sr., and Reverend Lawrence Gilmore.

You Are

You are my Hope
My joy and my rest
You are my wonderful counselor
My almighty God by whom I am blessed

You are my Jehovah Jireh
And so much more to me
You are the miracle that came in the flesh
For all the world to see

You are my rock of ages, my crown of glory
The one who wipes away my tears
You are my Comforter, the Holy One
Who calms all of my fears

You are Abba Father, my Lord
Who reached out and saved my soul
You are my sweet Jesus
The King that I long to behold

You are my water
When I thirst in a dry place
You are my direction when I am lost
I close my eyes and I see your face

You are my restoration,
The lifter up of my head
You are my blessed peace and quietness
Just like the Bible said

You are my burden bearer
And my ultimate healer
You are the eyes through which I see
Because you are my true revealer

You are my Balm of Gilead,
My brother and my friend
You are my Alpha and Omega
My beginning and my end

You are my breastplate of righteousness
And my strong tower
You are my help and my rock
You fill me with power

You are the Babe, the Christ child,
The horn of salvation
You are my precious and sweet Lord
The one who made all creation.

Exodus 3:14 (King James Version)
And God said unto Moses, I AM THAT I AM:
and he said, thus shalt thou say unto the
children of Israel, I AM hath sent me unto you.

My Inspiration for:
You Got to Make Room for Your Blessings

How many know, when your manager calls you into the office and closes the door it is normally NOT a good thing? Several years ago, I worked for a nonprofit. I loved that job and felt excited every day to get started.

When the director called me in her office and closed the door, I did not hear her actually say the words 'You're fired.' What I heard was that 'due to budget cuts my position would no longer be funded.'

Truly it was not a monetary loss, because when I looked at the number of hours I worked; at best I was earning about a nickel an hour! However, I was very personally invested in the mission to make a better community. I felt hurt and a little lost after the meeting. Ok, I said to myself, remain positive, don't let the fact you have a legally binding contract cause you to take a negative action.

God spoke to me and said 'let it go!' I immediately went by to see the program director just to say thank you for the opportunity to work on the community initiative.

I had recently retired from the federal government and the time I spent working with the non-profit was very rewarding. Oh, what to do now? That was seven years ago and since I 'let go and let God,' I have become a successful entrepreneur. The Lord has blessed me to provide jobs to hundreds of people over the past seven years. God's plan for my life with overflowing blessings started with me letting go and making room for those blessings.

Romans 8:28 notes, 'for we know that all things work together for good to them that love God, to them who are called according to his purpose.' God has given us a promise that He will work it out. Yet often, we grumble and complain instead of trusting and obeying God so that we might gain.

I am a living witness when we are down to nothing, God is up to something! Let no one deceive you, we are blessed and highly favored regardless of our situation. All we need to do is just keep looking up to Jesus the author and finisher of our faith! Won't He do it?? Yes, He will!!!!

Dedication: To those who have a heart to give, but don't have the resources ... have faith, believe, and know that there is a blessing on the way. Good measure pressed down, shaken together, and running over is in store for you!

You Gotta Make Room for Your Blessings

You gotta make room for your blessings
Get rid of stuff you don't need
Is what you holding on to something you can
use
If not, give it to someone and plant a positive
seed

You've been praying for God to bless you
But how do you handle what you've already
got
God can't fill what's already filled
Being a good steward is required whether you
want to or not

Try focusing on what you can do for others
If you want a testimony of miracles to confess
Watch and see his mighty works in your life
When you start praying, God who can I bless?

Deuteronomy 28:2 (King James Version)
And all these blessings shall come on thee,
and overtake thee, if thou shalt hearken unto
the voice of the LORD thy God.

My Inspiration for: The Past is the Past

I remember my past, but I don't live in it. I thank God for the past and I thank Him for the present. I also thank God for the future because He has a plan and purpose for my life and it is good.

The forgiveness and new life in Christ is freely given to all born again believers which places our past mistakes in the past.

However, it is amazing how long people will remember your mistakes. Twenty, 30, 40, or even 50 years may have passed and someone will remember and remind you of past mistakes.

I was having a conversation with a co-worker when she told me her pastor had been recently convicted of a crime he had committed more than 10 years ago. When she told me how the church reacted to the pastor, and his wife because of this conviction, I could not help but feel sad. As I stood there, the Lord spoke into my spirit for every mistake in my past; I was not given a parole – I was given a brand-new record! As the Holy Spirit ministered to me, I smiled as I thought about some recent events in my life.

I am a mother, a grandmother, and great-grandmother, yet someone brought up my past mistakes as a teenager. I thought about the goodness and mercy of God. I thought about my past and the mistakes I had made. Now, because of God wrapping himself up in flesh and giving the ultimate sacrifice, I know I am a new creature in Christ. Thank God for the blood of Jesus that covered me and gave me a new start. Jesus covered my transgressions and put them as far as the east is from the west. Thank God the past is just that … the past.

This poem is dedicated to all those walking in the mercy and forgiveness of Jesus Christ with a new walk, a new talk, a new day, a new beginning, and a new life. *Therefore if any man be in Christ, he is a new creature: old things are passed away; behold, all things are become new (King James Version).*

The Past is the Past

Your past mistakes in life
Don't guarantee what
your future is going to be
Jesus can make you brand new
Just like He did for others and like He did for
me

You see, I was once the woman
Whose back was surely bent
But I begged for God's mercy
And prayed that His healing power be sent

God looked at me and said
You are loosed forevermore
The fruits of the spirit await you
Just come and open the door

Just praise me in your circumstance
Praise me in your situation
Be thankful for the blood of Jesus
It is by Him that you and I are in relation

I sent my Son to set the captives free
To heal the sick and raise the dead
To confound the wise with all the miracles
And bruise the serpent's head

So although the road has been rough
I never lost faith in what God can do
In the beauty of His Holiness
I am thankful that His love is always true.

John 8: 4-7 (King James Version)
[4] They say unto him, Master, this woman was taken in adultery, in the very act.
[5] Now Moses in the law commanded us, that such should be stoned: but what sayest thou?
[6] This they said, tempting him, that they might have to accuse him. But Jesus stooped down, and with his finger wrote on the ground, as though he heard them not.
[7] So when they continued asking him, he lifted up himself, and said unto them, He that is without sin among you, let him first cast a stone.

My Inspiration for: Be Careful

Growing up as a child in North Carolina, my mother had a thousand things to share about being careful. I was told to be careful not to leave home with holes in my clothes, just in case I became ill and had to be taken to the hospital. I was told not to take money from people, because they may want something in return. I was told to be careful of the company I kept … 'birds of a feather flock together.' I was told to be careful crossing the street. I was told to be careful not to eat too much cranberry sauce, because my jaws would lock. It is funny now to remember how much time I spent opening and closing my mouth so I would avoid my jaws locking. As a child, I really believed her.! Only later did I find out this was my mama's way of making sure I didn't eat too much cranberry sauce. My mama told me to be careful not to be wasteful

... 'waste not, want not.' I was told to be careful to rise early because the early bird catches the worm (my thought as a child was did I really want a worm?).

For an extra added measure, mama even quoted Shakespeare, although I doubt she realized it was Shakespeare, "neither a borrower nor a lender be." My mama always seemed to time her little talks when I was in a hurry to go somewhere or had something else to do.

Unfortunately for me, not only did she want to share her pearls of wisdom, but there was always a long story and questions asked to make sure I understood. I learned early in life to listen and pay attention, so I didn't have to endure the pain of hearing the story twice! The list goes on and on and sometimes I was convinced my mama didn't sleep very much at night, because she was up thinking of new 'tidbits of wisdom' to share with me!

One day I broke one of the 'be carefuls' – neither a borrower or lender be. I loaned one of my classmates a white blouse. Believe me, that was a huge mistake, because my mama was meticulous about her laundry. All her white clothes were bleached and rinsed with bluing (a blue powder used to brighten white clothes). My mama's whites were bright-white and she beamed with pride when neighbors passed by and commented on her whiter-than-white clothes hanging on the clothes line.

As carefully as I tried to hide the (now returned, clean, but dingy white) blouse, it took my mama only about a half a second to spot it tucked away in my closet. Of course, what followed was something to be avoided ... the dreaded switch. In addition to the switch on my legs, I got the talk again about the ills of borrowing and lending. Needless to say, that ended my lending any clothes!

Years later, I still smile when my actions are inadvertently interrupted by a 'my mama told me to be careful' pause. I can hear her voice telling me to be careful.

As a child of God, I now know many of the things my mama shared with me about being careful were based on biblical principles because, yes, we do have to careful of our how we spend our time and with whom we spend it. We have to watch as well as pray, again, I say watch.

This poem is dedicated to the memory

of my late mama, Emma Windy Cinderella
Dorothy Bell Brown Pearson, known to all as
'Miss Dorothy Bell.'

Be Careful

Be Careful how you spend your time
Be careful who you call a friend
Be careful if you borrow
Be even more careful
If you decide to lend

Be careful how you use your gifts
Be careful what you believe
Be careful to speak life
Be even more careful
Because the devil's job is to deceive

Be careful to lay aside every weight and sin
Be careful how you run the race
Be careful how you chart your course
Be even more careful
So you won't end up in the wrong place!

Proverbs 13:20 (King James Version)
He that walketh with wise men shall be wise:
but a companion of fools shall be destroyed.

My Inspiration for:
God's Love Doesn't Let Go

On my left arm, I have a permanent scar. I have shown my scar to many people over the years. When I show it to them, I always press it so they can see it no longer hurts. Then I tell the story of when the scar was a fresh wound. It was so painful that even a slight breeze would make it hurt, and so deep a wound that it healed rather slowly. I show my scar and smile while letting the world know it is the evidence God healed me and He is still healing.

One of my most precious memories of showing my scar was to a cancer survivor. Due to the chemo treatments, his body was covered with growths on his face. I walked over to him and proudly showed him my scar and explained my story. I told him it was so beautiful to see the growths on his face. He looked at me and smiled, but had a questioning look on his face. I told him I loved seeing the growths on his face because that was the evidence to the world that God was healing him! God is telling the world "I love you and I have you in my healing hands. My power to heal is greater than any report the enemy can deliver."

We can identify with scars because we all have them. The scars of a painful past.

Some of those scars are unsightly and have caused us deep regret. It is such a blessing to know some of our deepest scars are reflective of just how determined God was to hold on to us and refused to let go.

I heard a story about a little boy who jumped in the lake for a swim. His mother looked out the window and saw an alligator swimming towards her son. The mother ran toward the water and yelled to warn her son. Hearing her voice, the little boy turned and began swimming to his mother. Just as he reached her, the alligator reached him.

From the dock, the mother grabbed her little boy by the arms just as the alligator snatched his legs. The alligator was much stronger than the mother, but the mother's love made her determined not to let go. A farmer driving by, heard her screams, raced from his truck, took aim and shot the alligator.

Remarkably, the little boy survived. His legs were extremely scarred by the vicious attack from the alligator and, on his arms were deep scratches where his mother's fingernails dug into his flesh in her effort to hang on to her son.

The newspaper reporter who interviewed the boy after the trauma, asked if the boy would show him his scars. The boy lifted his pant legs. Then with obvious pride, he said to the reporter, "But, look at my arms. I have great scars on my arms, too. I have them because my mom wouldn't let go."

I can identify with that little boy in how proud he was to show his scars. Just as his mother did not let go, so it is with God. He will never let go and we have the scars as evidence that He didn't!

In the midst of your struggle, He is there holding on to you. He did not, and will not, ever let you go. Be blessed as you read *God's Love Doesn't Let Go!*

This poem is dedicated to all who carry a scar which is the evidence that God heals. We are here today to show our scars because God didn't let go.

God's Love Doesn't Let Go

Hurtful words
mean and spiteful actions
Look at me, I've got so many wounds
and Lord knows I've got scratches

But thank God His love doesn't let go
It just keeps holding on

Though tears flood my eyes
Because of what you say and do
I stand firmly on God's word
Which is tried and true

But thank God His love doesn't let go It just
keeps holding on

You say things to hurt me
which are not even true
I'm too tired to fight back
Looking for rest and wondering what to do

But thank God His love doesn't let go It just
keeps holding on

You run and spread lies
Hoping your poison will hit its mark
You wait and hope to see my downfall
So that on a celebration you can embark

But thank God His love doesn't let go It just
keeps holding on

The ups and downs
Have been many too many to count
The broken promises and dreams
You tried to replace my hopes with despair
and doubt

But thank God His love doesn't let go
It just keeps holding on

Romans 8:37-39 (King James Version)
[37] Nay, in all these things we are more than conquerors through him that loved us.
[38] For I am persuaded, that neither death, nor life, nor angels, nor principalities, nor powers, nor things present, nor things to come,
[39] Nor height, nor depth, nor any other creature, shall be able to separate us from the love of God, which is in Christ Jesus our Lord.

My Inspiration for: Good Morning

After many years of working for the government, I was finally able to say, 'I no longer work for the Department of Defense (DoD), only GOD.' Praise God from whom all blessings flow. Waking up and looking out of the window, I realized the blessings of God were overflowing in my life. Yea, yea, God.

I then remembered my prayer petition before I retired. It was a question, 'God how do I redeem the time that you have given me?' You gave me an 'economic ministry' and the pathway has been nothing short of a miracle. By your grace and your mercy, you have given me the opportunity to 'sow and water' in the lives of others. I thank you God. Thank you for ordering my footsteps. Thank you for every morning that presents a new opportunity to give you praise, honor, and glory. Thank you for every morning you wake me up and allow me to be a blessing to others. Thank you for reminding me, when I see a need, you are not holding me accountable for what I cannot do ... only for what I can do.

This poem is dedicated to those who have hearts overflowing with love that bring sunshine into the lives of others.

Good Morning

This morning when I woke up
You kissed me with the sun
I began to pray and thank You
For all that You have done

A smile crossed my face
As I thought about my situation
The blessings and benefits that come
With just being Your creation!

Proverbs 10:22 (King James Version)
The blessing of the LORD, it maketh rich, and
he addeth no sorrow with it.

My Inspiration for: Your Friend

Years ago, I was traveling from North Carolina to my daughter's home with her grandmother Miss Essie Lee. I had known Mrs. Essie Lee Hill McMillan all my life, and true to 'southern tradition,' I called her Miss Essie Lee. As we were traveling, I started to hum and sing. I was unaware I was singing. I was just driving along and I guess a song was in my spirit.

Miss Essie Lee said, "I have known you all of your life and I have never heard you sing!"

I smiled and replied, "I guess I never had anything to sing about."

Truly when you have the joy of the Lord and you have received the spirit of adoption whereby you may cry Abba Father; you just feel like singing. You not only want to sing, but you want to bless the name of the Lord and tell the world ... come see a man who told me everything I ever did! I have a friend that sticketh closer than a brother and his name is Jesus.

This poem is dedicated to friendships new and old. Che trova un amico trova un Tesoro; an Italian proverb translated as: He who finds a friend finds a treasure.

Your Friend

What the devil meant for bad
God said I have a good expected end
Call on Me, my beloved
I am your Savior and your friend!

Proverbs 18:24 (King James Version)
A man friends must shew himself friendly: and
there is a friend sticketh closer than a brother.

My Inspiration for:
You Have Been Considered

When Reverend Daffin of Mt. Olive Baptist Church of Centerville, Virginia began to preach, I found myself yielding and saying, yes, Lord. Her sermon came from the book of Job and the sermon topic … *You Have Been Considered*.

The word of God came forth and my dear sister began to boldly declare that as children of the most-high King we should be joyful that God will consider us. Just as God asked Satan, "have you considered my servant Job?", we should welcome the times when God will ask if Satan will consider us. Why, would be want to go through the trials and tribulations that Job endured? For one thing, it is through trials and tribulations that we are revived and refined so we may have a testimony of victory.

Secondly, we become a living testimony to the world that we are God's divine workmanship, and we are fearfully and wonderfully made by Him. Having on our spiritual armor, we are battlefield ready and equipped to fight the good fight of faith.

From the book of Job, we hear from God that Satan does not have power or authority over us. We can be confident because God tells us that NOTHING can happen unless He will permit, allow or ordain it. Praise God from whom all blessings flow.

This poem is dedicated to Reverend Elizabeth Ann Daffin, Mt. Olive Baptist Church, Centreville, Virginia.

You Have Been Considered

Casting all your care upon Him
Because He cares for you
Wait on the Lord
And your strength He will renew

When you are in doubt
About which way to go and what to do
All you need to remember
Are the promises that God has given you

Don't ever forget
That satan desires to sift you as wheat
His tricks are cunning
And full of deceit

God has considered you
And let you be put to the test
He picked you
Because you are one of His best

Satan can't do anything
That God does not allow
Hold fast to your faith
Keep your hand on the gospel plow

It is a battle of the mind
And the flesh that you must overcome
But just walk in the spirit
Through Jesus, the victory is already won!

Job 1:8 (King James Version)
And the LORD said unto Satan, Hast thou
considered my servant Job, that there is none
like him in the earth, a perfect and an upright
man, one that feareth God, and escheweth
evil? Only upon himself put not forth thine
hand. So, Satan went forth from the presence
of the LORD.

My Inspiration for:
You Will Live and Not Die

I listened to the story of faith, love, and victory. Bishop Jessie Williams spoke softly telling me of the time he spent in a coma for over a month. As he slept, days and then weeks passed. The doctors told his daughter his condition would not improve. They also told his daughter by some chance, if he should live, he would be a vegetable – unable to think, speak, or walk.

The only recourse was to remove the Bishop from life support, which was – in their words – only prolonging the inevitable. But, God, unbeknownst to the doctor, spoke to Bishop and said, 'I am sending you back … there is more work for you to do.' God said, 'you shall live and not die.' Now several years later, Bishop is still preaching, teaching, encouraging, and winning souls.

There is a similar story of victory in Jesus from my sister in Christ, Reverend Rose McIrath Slade, who has had many battles that man thought was the end, but God said, 'no Rose, I want you to continue your work.' My Rose continues to be battlefield ready and always has a prayer and a praise for the Lord.

This poem is dedicated to Bishop Jessie Williams, Reverend Rose McElrath-Slade, and everyone that was given a notice by man it was the end, and God said you *will* live and not die.

You Will Live and Not Die

The enemy walked away
And left you for dead
But hallelujah God spoke a word
And here is what He said

You have been wounded my child
And the wounds are very deep
But remember Psalms 23
When you prayed my soul to keep

Now I will do a miracle
For my name's sake
And this day your life
The enemy will not take

You will live and not die
So that My works you will declare
You will aid the widows and orphans
And minister to those in despair

In your heart I hid My word
It is planted on fertile ground
Arise and go tell a dying world
Seek the Lord, while He may be found!

Psalm 118:17 (King James Version)
I shall not die, but live, and declare the works
of the LORD.

My Inspiration for: Blessings

As I think about the awesome blessings of God and His plan of favor, I remember the story of Naomi. Naomi's circumstances caused her to became poor and a childless widow. Naomi had suffered losses so great she even changed her name from Naomi, meaning 'pleasantness,' to Mara meaning 'bitter'; but God had a plan of prosperity and purpose for her life.

As in Naomi's situation, we can often feel a sense of despair when we have suffered loss. A single mother or father trying to make it on one income, a widow or widower trying to make it alone, or a child abandoned by both mother and father – all cry out to God in utter despair. Though it can look hopeless, remember Naomi's blessings did not come from what she had, but from the favor and blessings that God caused to flow to Naomi through her daughter-in-law, Ruth. Ruth had found favor and was blessed by a near kinsman of Naomi, named Boaz. It is beautiful to see how the blessings flowed from God to Boaz, then Boaz to Ruth, and lastly from Ruth to Naomi.

This poem is dedicated to everyone who has grown weary amidst their struggle. We serve a God that will give us blessings that will overtake us.

Blessings

You see I am living in a house
That I didn't build
It is filled with things
That I didn't buy

I have trees
That I didn't plant
All I did was release my faith
And give Jesus a try!

Deuteronomy 28:1-2 (King James Version)
[1] And it shall come to pass, if thou shalt hearken diligently unto the voice of the LORD thy God, to observe and to do all his commandments which I command thee this day, that the LORD thy God will set thee on high above all nations of the earth:
[2] And all these blessings shall come on thee, and overtake thee, if thou shalt hearken unto the voice of the LORD thy God.

My Inspiration for: A Little Advice

Advice is something people freely offer. Unlike other things closely held, advice is given generously. Advice, however, falls into what I have described to my grandchildren as my 'corn on the cob category.'

Are you wondering what corn-on-the-cob has to do with advice? It is very simple. God has given all of us enough sense to eat the corn, which is the good part, and throw the cob away – which is not useful for consumption.

We have so many different types of advice. We have a little advice, we have sage advice, we have friendly advice, we have loving advice, and we have strong advice. We get advice from our parents, our spouses, our family, our friends, our teachers, and sometimes we even find ourselves giving advice to ourselves.

At the end of the day regardless of the type of advice or who gives you the advice, it will take you back to my corn-on-the-cob theory ... use what is good and throw the rest away. So, this little advice is from a friend, and I pray you will use what is good for you and throw the rest away!

This poem is dedicated to mothers ... who always have advice ... it's in their DNA!

A Little Advice

You look over the situation
Thinking about how your ends don't meet
When it comes to worry
You always take a front row seat

Listen carefully my friend
While you're sitting on the front row
It's time to gain understanding
Of just how to prosper and grow

The key is to follow Bible principles
Realize God has cattle on a thousand hills
You were not made to be in bondage
Nor to spend all your money paying bills

Start to plan ahead
Of what you will buy and when
Remember the lust of the eye
Can be a terrible sin

Every time you want to borrow
Decide is it a want or a need
Look carefully on the long-term effects
Is it worth it indeed?

James 1:17 (King James Version)
Every good gift and every perfect gift is from
above, and cometh down from the Father of
lights, with whom is no variableness, neither
shadow of turning.

My Inspiration for: Release Your Faith

My life has had many turns, ups and downs. There were times I was low on funds, food, and friends, but the one thing I have always had is faith. Because I am housed in an earthly vessel, there have been times my faith was that of a mustard seed, but the bible says that is all we need. I have always believed God at his word ... that what He sent it to do, that it would not return void. There are times that my faith has caused people to look at me as if I have lost my mind.

One such example is when I cried out to the Lord after losing my husband. The Lord told me to get ready. That was on a Saturday. On the following Monday, I called my manager and told her I would not be in for a few days.

My manager told me to take the week off because I had not taken any time off since my husband had passed. I took the week off and began to get ready. I sorted, discarded, and donated. Of course, with all this activity, my neighbors began inquiring what was going on.

I told them I was getting ready to move. Of course, the natural questions came, when was I moving? I responded … "I don't know." The next question, where am I moving to? I responded, "I don't know." The only thing I could tell them was I was getting ready to move. The puzzled looks on the faces from those that inquired were priceless.

That was June. In October, I moved from Virginia Beach to Japan! Truly faith is the substance of things hoped for … the evidence of things not seen. For that reason, in faith I had a moving company pack boxes and label them for the garage when I did not have a garage or even a house. Yet in faith, when I opened the boxes, I opened them in my garage.

In faith, the first time I traveled to Africa, I did not have hotel reservations. Yet in faith I was received in the home of a family who loved and cared for me as a family member. In faith, I built a home from the ground up in a town I had never been to and never visited.

Not once did I even go there while the construction was taking place. The Lord said to wait and I did. When I traveled there for the first time, I had to use GPS to locate the town!

Do I recommend these things to you? No. This was what God had spoken to ME and He fulfilled His promises. When God speaks, I move just like that. Know His voice and when He speaks I move in faith.

My poem is dedicated to faith walkers … remain fully confident that what God says, He is not only able, He will bring it to pass.

Release Your Faith

If He is an all sufficient God
Able to supply all of your need
It doesn't matter what remains in your hand
Release your faith and plant a positive seed!

Philippians 4:19 (King James Version)
But my God shall supply all your need
according to his riches in glory by Christ
Jesus.

Inspiration for: You Showed Us

The late Reverend Otis Williams was such a wonderful, loving, and caring man. As I think about him now, I can hear him saying, "how are you doing 'darling?'" It made me feel special, but then again, that was Reverend Williams. He had a way of making everyone feel special and loved! Though we all knew that he called all the women 'darling,' we always greeted him back with a smile, and walked away feeling special. One of the most beautiful things about it was everyone, and I mean everyone, knew there was only one 'heartbeat of love' for Reverend Williams and that was his beloved wife, Deaconess Tina.

As he came in and out of our lives based on his assignments from God, we were sad to see him go and rejoicing to see him return. During the last months of his life, we watched as he bravely and lovingly continued to work for the Lord. He could be counted on to be there. He could be counted on to greet you with a smile. If he was not having a good day, we certainly didn't know it. Oh, how we loved him and we were truly blessed, because he loved us back.

On the evening after his funeral I sat on the side of my bed. As I sat there thinking about my wonderful friend, words began to flow like the tears that washed my face. I was hurting, I was crying and yet I found myself smiling as I scribbled the words about my friend, Reverend Otis Williams. Be blessed as you read about my friend whom God called from labor to reward … *You Showed Us*.

This poem is dedicated in memory of the late Reverend Otis Williams and his legacy of love.

You Showed Us

You showed us that
it is for God we must live
You showed us by example
to give the best that we have to give

You showed us how to climb mountains
with a smile on our face
You showed us that it is important
not only to run but to finish the race

You showed us how to be faithful
over what we do for the master
You showed us how to keep moving forward
even in the face of disaster

You showed us how
to always treat everyone with love
You showed us how
to set our affections on things above

You showed us how
to be faithful in what we do and say
You showed us how
to cherish each other in every way

You showed us the meaning
of how a real soldier must stand
You showed us how to live God's word
and take possession of the land

You showed us how to fight the good fight
even when your health failed
You showed us that you were battlefield ready
… you would not be derailed

You showed us commitment to Christ
and determination to stand
You showed us there is a Lily in the valley
and you were holding His hand

You showed us how to sing with joy
even near the close of the day
You showed us how to keep moving …
never losing sight of the straight and narrow
way

You showed us how to see the sunshine
in the midst of a stormy sky
You showed us how to have a joyful melody
even when it was time to say goodbye

You showed us how to live
and yes you even showed us how to die
You showed us how to accept it all
never asking why

You showed us that you lived your life
according to the master plan
You showed us my brother
that you were God's man!

2 Timothy 4:7 (King James Version)
... have fought a good fight, I have finished
my course, I have kept the faith:

Inspiration for:
Every Burden Is a Blessing

Praying for a burden? I tried as hard as I could in my sanctified, holy, sold-out-for-Jesus, I am on my way to heaven, no-cross-no-crown mind, to understand and yet nothing came to mind. I could not understand why my spiritual father and Pastor, Bishop Jesse Williams told us we needed to pray and ask God to give us a burden.

As much as I tried, I was like my youngest granddaughter when asked to give a few words at the family dinner, she shrugged her shoulders, and said, "I got nothing!"

Standing there with the rest of the saints, I tried my best not to reveal I didn't get it. Feeling it would absolutely be 'un-Christian' of me to question Bishop about why we should ask for a burden, I left saying, 'Lord speak to me and give me the meaning of this.'

Days, weeks, months and years passed … almost 10 years to be exact … before I 'got it.'

It came to me … not in prayer service, bible study, or morning worship … I was alone on a freezing cold day in a storage unit packing clothing, toys, and books for a missionary trip to Nigeria. It was almost 2:00 in the afternoon and I had been in the freezing cold storage unit since about 9:00 in the morning.

I thought about all the people who had volunteered to help me … and yet not one single person came. Not that I blamed them for sitting in a warm home with family and friends enjoying a nice, tasty Thanksgiving dinner. The option of helping someone pack and load boxes in a freezing cold storage unit versus a warm dinner with family made it a pretty easy decision.

I began to cry, softly at first, and then louder and louder. Then I began to dance my holy dance and lift my hands in praise. I began to say over and over, 'Lord I thank you.' I finally realized the Lord had given me a burden. A burden was on my heart for the little orphans in Nigeria. So, the word from the Lord that Bishop Williams had spoken many years ago came to me … I finally got it.

I had a burden given to me by the Lord Himself. Therefore, in spite of the cold, in spite of the labor, in spite of the people who did not come, I was there rejoicing and praising God.

I had a burden and I was not weary. I had a burden and I was not tired. I had a burden and I was not discouraged. I had a burden and I was not disappointed. I had a burden of love for children that did not even know my name, yet my heart was overflowing with joy.

Lord, in your own time you let me know that *every* burden is a blessing!

This poem is dedicated those that have prayed and God has granted your prayer petition and given you a burden.

Every Burden Is a Blessing

Every burden is a blessing
regardless of what my eyes may see
Every burden is a blessing
because my heavenly Father is watching over
me

Every burden is a blessing
no matter what may come my way
Every burden is a blessing
because to Him I can always pray

Every burden is a blessing
even when I see little good and much that is
bad
Every burden is a blessing
because He makes my joy full even when I'm
sad

Every burden is a blessing
when my heart aches and tears fill my eyes
Every burden is a blessing
because Jesus promised He will hear my cries

Every burden is a blessing
even when I face challenges day by day
Every burden is a blessing
because there's no problem God can't move
out of my way

Every burden is a blessing
even when troubles surround me on every
hand
Every burden is a blessing
because in faith it is on the solid rock I shall
stand!

Galatians 6:2 (King James Version)
Bear ye one another's burdens, and so fulfil
the law of Christ.

Inspiration for: I See Too Many

I sit quietly and listen to words that pierce my heart. I watch as the tears well up in his eyes, as my friend tells me his story of a broken relationship. Not with his wife, not with his children, not with a family member, or a friend, but with his church. If this was the first time I had heard the story, it would different.

Sadly, it is a story that I have heard too many times over the years. I have heard the story from church-members, non-members, deacons, ushers, trustees and, yes, even preachers. The locations and the names are different but the stories are the same ... hurt and wounded inside the church.

How does this happen and what do we do about it? How can we, as loving ambassadors of Christ, stop the chain-of-hurt that prevents us from accomplishing our true, meaningful, and purpose driven mission –

which is to spread the good news of Jesus Christ.

How do we get to the place in Jesus where His love is overflowing in our lives? How do we get to the place where His love in us draws others to Him? How do we get to the place where we feel the hurt and pain of our brother and sister when no words are spoken? How do we get to that place where we have and take time to help each other? How do we get to that place where our thoughts are loving, our hugs are comforting and our words are encouraging?

Maybe, just maybe if we would have the loving heart of Christ to simply love each other, not for who we are, but whose we are; love will overflow and change in the church will happen.

This poem is dedicated to all those with hearts overflowing with love.

I See Too Many

I see too many hurting and too many broken
I see the look....no words have to be spoken
I see too much loneliness and too much
despair
I see too many faces that tell me that there is
no one to care

I see too many sad eyes welled up with tears
I see too many pressed down by doubts and
fears
I see too many shut out for one reason or
another
I see too many longing for the comfort of sister
or a brother

I see too many walking out the same way that
they came in
I see too many overcome by the battle they
feel they can't win
I see too many tired of waiting for a broken
heart to mend

I see too many that are in need of a kind and
encouraging word from a friend

I see too many! I see you!
I see me!

1 Peter 3:8-9 (King James Version)
[8] Finally, be ye all of one mind, having
compassion one of another, love as brethren,
be pitiful, be courteous:
[9] Not rendering evil for evil, or railing for
railing: but contrariwise blessing; knowing that
ye are thereunto called, that ye should inherit
a blessing.

Inspiration for: Write it Down

At a women's retreat I heard what I would call a 'stick to your ribs' message. Sometimes when you hear this type of wisdom, it may be several hours after you have heard it that the Holy Spirit reveals the complete message. As Dr. Kimberly Walston stood to speak, I saw a beautiful and powerful young woman of God. I saw a woman preaching in power who – only hours earlier – been flat on her back in the hospital.

I saw a woman who did not look like she had been through all of the recent hard trials she shared with us. I saw a woman who had been told by doctors in a few short years she would not be able to walk or even feed herself.

Dr. Walston said she learned how to push past her problems and struggles and gain power by writing down God's sweet blessings. As God told Moses to write it down as a memorial and rehearse it, so did Dr.

Walston write it down as a memorial and rehearse it. Dr. Walston even had a small box she used to hold memories of her special remembrances and celebrations as her own personal memorial.

As I drove home later that evening my mind shifted to thoughts of things to do before going to bed. It was Thursday night and I needed to place the trash outside. I walked in the house to grab the bag and instantly the Lord started speaking to me. I grabbed a paper towel and started writing as the Lord was speaking to me ... write it down. The trash never went out that night, but my soul was blessed all over again with the thoughts of writing down the memorial.

This poem is dedicated to Dr. Kimberly Walston.

Write It Down

Write it down as a memorial
The things that I've done for you
Write it down so you will remember
What I've brought you through

Write it down so that when tears wash your
face
And you can't even pray
Write it down so you will remember
New mercies I will bring each and every day

Write it down so you will remember
When you're too tired to fight
Write it down so you will remember
What the devil meant for bad I made it alright

Write it down so you will remember
I touched your body and by faith you were
healed
Write it down so that you will remember
Even through your trials My power was
revealed

Write it down
Remember it
And rehearse it in your mind
Write it down
Remember it
Because My love for you
Is one of a kind.

Exodus 17:14 (King James Version)
And the LORD said unto Moses, Write this for
a memorial in a book, and rehearse it in the
ears of Joshua: for I will utterly put out the
remembrance of Amalek from under heaven.

Inspiration for: Let Me Be the One

As a child, do you remember when you wanted to be the first one selected for the softball team? Do you remember when the teacher asked you to get in line and you wanted to be the first one? Remember when you were trying to be first to play jump rope? Remember when you were asked that famous question … who wants ice cream?

Can you remember you hand waving wildly in the air while you gleefully shouted me, me, me! You were so happy and excited because you had chance to be the one. There may have been others, but you wanted to be the one.

Do you also remember how excited you were when you started your relationship with Jesus? You were bubbling over with joy and you wanted to tell everyone about your savior, your friend, your advocate, your comforter, and your provider.

If someone wanted to know about Him, you were ready any time day or night to share the gospel. You were ready to go anywhere to give witness of your risen Savior.

Sitting at my computer looking at the 'refresh' button, I started to think about that feeling. It is time for us to hit the refresh button and go back to the time we bubbled over with joy when given the opportunity to spread the good news of Jesus Christ. We need to go back to the time when we always had a praise and a testimony. Are you raising your hand now? Do you want to be the one? Are you saying me, me, me? I want to be the one Jesus to remember your love and share it with the world. I want to be the one to lift you up so that you will draw all men unto you.

This poem is dedicated to a few that raised their hands and said, "me Lord"; Dr. Cathy C. Jones, Bishop Wallace Grimes, Reverend Mark Akinosho, and the late Deacon Morris Leon Churchill, Sr.

Let Me Be the One

Let me be the one to remember
all that You've done
Let me be the one to say thank you for
sending Your only begotten Son

Let me be the one who holds fast
to the promises that you've made
Let me be the one to tell the world
of the ultimate sacrifice that You gave

Let me be the one that lives for You
no matter what others may do or say
Let me be the one that is always filled with joy
at the end of each and every day

Let me be the one that will find peace and rest
at my journey's end
Let me be the one to hear the words well done
… from Jesus my Savior and my friend!

Matthew 25:33-40

[33] And he shall set the sheep on his right hand, but the goats on the left.

[34] Then shall the King say unto them on his right hand, Come, ye blessed of my Father, inherit the kingdom prepared for you from the foundation of the world:

[35] For I was an hungred, and ye gave me meat: I was thirsty, and ye gave me drink: I was a stranger, and ye took me in:

[36] Naked, and ye clothed me: I was sick, and ye visited me: I was in prison, and ye came unto me.

[37] Then shall the righteous answer him, saying, Lord, when saw we thee an hungred, and fed thee? or thirsty, and gave thee drink?

[38] When saw we thee a stranger, and took thee in? or naked, and clothed thee?

[39] Or when saw we thee sick, or in prison, and came unto thee?

[40] And the King shall answer and say unto them, Verily I say unto you, inasmuch as ye have done it unto one of the least of these my brethren, ye have done it unto me.

My Prayer

God give me a sound mind
Lord God, Father of Abraham, Isaac and
Jacob
Give me contentment, peace, and joy
Give me understanding
So that I may know You even the more

Lord, order my steps by Your word
I want to do Your will
Touch my heart so that when I speak
Words of love and encouragement will flow
Give me the opportunity
to be a blessing in someone's life!
In Jesus Name Amen

My Commitment: Here I am Lord, Send Me!

About *Corliss A. Udoema*

The author is a preacher, evangelist, missionary, workshop facilitator, entrepreneur, and writer. Most of all she loves the Lord and prays continuously for opportunities to lift the name of Jesus. Since early childhood, she has used her gifts of exhortation and helps to reach out to those in need. God has blessed Udoema to travel to 59 countries (and islands), where she ministered, encouraged, and told the good news of Jesus.

She is an internationally accomplished motivational speaker and workshop facilitator. Over the past 35 years, Udoema has developed and facilitated many contract workshops, federal women workshops, budget workshops as well as religious retreats. She has served as key-note speaker and workshop facilitator for many government, non-profit, and faith based organizations including the General State Baptist Convention of North Carolina, Wyeth, and the North Carolina Continuing Education for Community Colleges Convention. She is the recipient of two Congressional awards for her work in the small business development area.

She is a life-long community worker and has been recognized for her contributions to assist and improve the quality of life and foster spiritual growth for those in need. She has served as a volunteer at Johnston Lee-Harnett Community Action where she taught budgeting and financial literacy classes.

Udoema is President of Agape Love in Action, Inc.(ALIA), a 501(c)(3) non-profit organization that reaches out to spread God's message of love by helping those in need. Most recently, Udoema has been involved with ALIA philanthropic efforts including 'Hope in a Bag,' which provides support and services to homeless shelter residents in Prince William County and Wisdom Meets Technology which provides computer literacy training and computers to senior citizens.

She was educated in the public schools of New Bern, NC and attended the University of Maryland. In the church at an early age, she has carried on the work of an evangelist and a missionary her entire life, and on October 2002, accepted the call into the ministry. On July 13, 2003, Udoema started preaching at her home church in New Bern, NC, Mt. Calvary Missionary Baptist Church where her former pastor, Dr. C. D. Bell presided.

Udoema retired from the Federal Government where she spent almost 33 years in various executive positions in contracting, grants, and procurement. Since 2006, she has served as CEO and President of her own international staffing and consulting company, Contract Solutions, Inc.

CHARITIES

Agape Love in Action (ALIA), Inc.

ALIA's mission is to help those in need. Motivated by faith, ALIA serves alongside the poor and oppressed as a demonstration of God's unconditional love for all people. ALIA, supports several outreach initiatives that include, Hope in a Bag, Wisdom Meets Technology, Business Battle Buddy, and Reach 2 Feed. In addition, ALIA sponsors community outreach and development programs which bring together local service providers and the people in the community who require assistance. ALIA endeavors to address the physical, emotional, mental, social, and economic wholeness in individuals, which impacts families and changes communities. ALIA works collaboratively with faith-based, philanthropic, government, corporate, academic, and community service organizations to meet the basic human needs of all people by providing tools to enhance whole lives.

For more information:
http://agapeloveinaction.com/

Lott Carey Global Christian Missional Community

The Mission of the Lott Carey Global Christian Missional Community extends the Christian witness around the world. Through prayer partnership, financial support, and technical assistance, we come alongside indigenous communities to support ministries of evangelism, compassion, empowerment, and advocacy. Together, we are touching lives with transforming love.

For more information:
http://lottcarey.org/

About the Book

The author speaks to us with words that have not come quickly nor easily. Each poem, each story, each miracle, each blessing and each revelation in A Guiding Light: Poems and Reflections was given to the author by the inspiration of the Holy Spirit. Over a span of more than 25 years while traveling to 59 countries, the author listened to God and with loving obedience wrote the words to each poem. Poems were written on notebook paper, napkins, paper bags, and even torn cardboard boxes, but one thing was consistent about each writing, they all came as one complete thought.

From the beginning to the end, the words flowed like a river. In this book, you see the heart of the author and her love for the Lord. In a warm and conversational style that is reflective of her childhood in New Bern, North Carolina, the author opens her heart to share miracles, stories of love, hope, joy, and peace in her walk of faith. Finally, the author shares her faith and stories from her childhood, as well as lessons learned in life, to produce a beautiful, inspirational, and free-verse book of poems. Read along as the author explains her inspiration for each poem in each stand-alone story while giving praises to her Lord and Savior, Jesus Christ.

The generous amount of white space in the book offers the reader space to write notes of their own. The text is 14-point font assisting those who need large text to read the inspirational and uplifting messages.

Made in the USA
San Bernardino, CA
03 January 2017